CENTRAL ISSUES IN CONTEMPORARY ECONOMIC THEORY AND POLICY

General Editor: **Gustavo Piga**, *Managing Editor, Rivista di Politica Economica, Rome, Italy*

Published titles include:

Mario Baldassarri, Luigi Paganetto and Edmund S. Phelps (*editors*)
INTERNATIONAL ECONOMIC INTERDEPENDENCE, PATTERNS OF TRADE BALANCES
AND ECONOMIC POLICY COORDINATION

Mario Baldassarri (*editor*)
KEYNES AND THE ECONOMIC POLICIES OF THE 1980s

Mario Baldassarri (*editor*)
OLIGOPOLY AND DYNAMIC COMPETITION

Mario Baldassarri (*editor*)
THE ITALIAN ECONOMY
Heaven or Hell?

Mario Baldassarri and Paolo Annunziato (*editors*)
IS THE ECONOMIC CYCLE STILL ALIVE?
Theory, Evidence and Policies

Mario Baldassarri, John McCallum and Robert A. Mundell (*editors*)
DEBT, DEFICIT AND ECONOMIC PERFORMANCE

Mario Baldassarri, John McCallum and Robert A. Mundell (*editors*)
GLOBAL DISEQUILIBRIUM IN THE WORLD ECONOMY

Mario Baldassarri and Robert A. Mundell (*editors*)
BUILDING THE NEW EUROPE VOLS I & II

Mario Baldassari (*editor*)
PRIVATIZATION PROCESSES IN EASTERN EUROPE
Theoretical Foundations and Empirical Results (Vols I & II)

Mario Baldassarri (*editor*)
HOW TO REDUCE UNEMPLOYMENT IN EUROPE

Mario Baldassarri (*editor*)
THE NEW WELFARE
Unemployment and Social Security in Europe

Mario Baldassarri, Michele Bagella and Luigi Paganetto (*editors*)
FINANCIAL MARKETS
Imperfect Information and Risk Management

Mario Baldassarri and Bruno Chiarini (*editors*)
STUDIES IN LABOUR MARKETS AND INDUSTRIAL RELATIONS

Mario Baldassarri and Pierluigi Ciocca (*editors*)
ROOTS OF THE ITALIAN SCHOOL OF ECONOMICS AND FINANCE
From Ferrara (1857) to Einaudi (1944) (three volumes)

Mario Baldassarri, Massimo Di Matteo and Robert A. Mundell (*editors*)
INTERNATIONAL PROBLEMS OF ECONOMIC INTERDEPENDENCE

Mario Baldassarri, Cesare Imbriani and Dominick Salvatore (*editors*)
THE INTERNATIONAL SYSTEM BETWEEN NEW INTEGRATION AND
NEO-PROTECTIONISM

Mario Baldassarri and Luca Lambertini (*editors*)
ANTITRUST, REGULATION AND COMPETITION

Mario Baldassarri, Alfredo Macchiati and Diego Piacentino (*editors*)
THE PRIVATIZATION OF PUBLIC UTILITIES
The Case of Italy

Mario Baldassarri, Luigi Paganetto and Edmund S. Phelps (*editors*)
EQUITY, EFFICIENCY AND GROWTH
The Future of the Welfare State

Mario Baldassarri, Luigi Paganetto and Edmund S. Phelps (*editors*)
THE 1990s SLUMP
Causes and Cures

Mario Baldassarri, Luigi Paganetto and Edmund S. Phelps (*editors*)
WORLD SAVING, PROSPERITY AND GROWTH

Mario Baldassarri, Luigi Paganetto and Edmund S. Phelps (*editors*)
INTERNATIONAL DIFFERENCES IN GROWTH RATES
Market Globalization and Economic Areas

Mario Baldassarri and Paolo Roberti (*editors*)
FISCAL PROBLEMS IN THE SINGLE-MARKET EUROPE

Mario Baldassarri and Franco Modigliani (*editors*)
THE ITALIAN ECONOMY
What Next?

Mario Baldassarri (*editor*)
MAFFEO PANTALEONI
At the Origin of the Italian School of Economics and Finance

Mario Baldassarri, Luigi Paganetto and Edmund S. Phelps (*editors*)
INSTITUTIONS AND ECONOMIC ORGANIZATION IN THE ADVANCED ECONOMIES
The Governance Perspective

Geoffrey Brennan (*editor*)
COERCIVE POWER AND ITS ALLOCATION IN THE EMERGENT EUROPE

Guido Cozzi and Roberto Cellini *(editors)*
INTELLECTUAL PROPERTY, COMPETITION, AND GROWTH

Debora Di Gioacchino, Sergio Ginebri and Laura Sabani *(editors)*
THE ROLE OF ORGANIZED INTEREST GROUPS IN POLICY MAKING

Luca Lambertini (*editor*)
FIRMS' OBJECTIVES AND INTERNAL ORGANISATION IN A GLOBAL ECONOMY
Positive and Normative Analysis

Riccardo Leoni and Giuseppe Usai *(editors)*
ORGANIZATIONS TODAY

Marco Malgarini and Gustavo Piga *(editors)*
CAPITAL ACCUMULATION, PRODUCTIVITY AND GROWTH
Monitoring Italy 2005

Stefano Manzocchi (*editor*)
THE ECONOMICS OF ENLARGEMENT

Gustavo Piga and Khi V. Thai
THE ECONOMICS OF PUBLIC PROCUREMENT

Central Issues in Contemporary Economic Theory and Policy
Series Standing Order ISBN 978–0–333–71464–5
(*outside North America only*)

You can receive future titles in this series as they are published by placing a standing order. Please contact your bookseller or, in case of difficulty, write to us at the address below with your name and address, the title of the series and the ISBN quoted above.

Customer Services Department, Macmillan Distribution Ltd, Houndmills, Basingstoke, Hampshire RG21 6XS, England

---

Firms' Objectives and Internal Organisation in a Global Economy

Positive and Normative Analysis

Edited by

Luca Lambertini

palgrave
macmillan

First published 2009 by
PALGRAVE MACMILLAN

Palgrave Macmillan in the UK is an imprint of Macmillan Publishers Limited, registered in England, company number 785998, of Houndmills, Basingstoke, Hampshire RG21 6XS.

Palgrave Macmillan in the US is a division of St Martin's Press LLC, 175 Fifth Avenue, New York, NY 10010.

Palgrave Macmillan is the global academic imprint of the above companies and has companies and representatives throughout the world.

Palgrave® and Macmillan® are registered trademarks in the United States, the United Kingdom, Europe and other countries.

ISBN-13: 978–0–230–22927–3   hardback

This book is printed on paper suitable for recycling and made from fully managed and sustained forest sources. Logging, pulping and manufacturing processes are expected to conform to the environmental regulations of the country of origin.

A catalogue record for this book is available from the British Library.

A catalog record for this book is available from the Library of Congress.

10   9   8   7   6   5   4   3   2   1
18   17   16   15   14   13   12   11   10   09

Printed and bound in Great Britain by
CPI Antony Rowe, Chippenham and Eastbourne

Contents

Preface

Luca Lambertini*
University of Bologna and University of Amsterdam

Whether firms indeed behave so as to maximize profits is a long standing issue in industrial economics, as testified by several classical contributions dating back to the late '50s and '60s, well before the game theory revolution that has generated the New Industrial Economics, now known as Theory of Industrial Organization. That early debate, now alas almost forgotten, discussed the possibility for firms to maximize the growth rate, the volume of sales, or revenues, instead of profits (see Baumol, 1958; Marris, 1953; Penrose, 1959; Williamson, 1966; and Solow, 1971). A parallel but completely independent stream of literature focused upon labour-managed firms (Ward, 1958; Vanek, 1977; Ireland and Law, 1982), or — almost equivalently — workers' enterprises (Sertel, 1982; Aoki, 1984), whose objective is the maximization of value added per worker, and/or profit sharing. Relatively later, the theory of strategic delegation has revived the interest for the idea that managerial firms may actually aim at maximizing a combination of profits and sales (Vickers, 1985) or profits and revenues (Fershtman and Judd, 1987).

After approximately two decades of globalization, the issue of defining firms' objectives has come back to the fore once again, strictly entangled with the companion issue of outsourcing vs vertical integration (see McLaren, 2000; Grossman and Helpman, 2002, inter alia). In a nutshell, the problem boils down to determining jointly the internal structure of the firm and its long-

* <luca.lambertini@unibo.it>, Department of Economics.

run investment projects in new products and technologies, in relation with the global market where specialized labour or capital inputs can be sought for outside the firm itself and even outside the country of residence of the firm. This clearly implies that globalization is not just a matter of free trade. It has expanded the set of possibilities made available to any given firm but it has also increased the competitive pressure to which the firm is exposed, along several dimensions.

The papers presented herewith revisit the theme of defining firms' objectives in the comparatively new perspective shaped by globalization. Far from pretending to be exhaustive, this collection of original studies aims at providing the reader with some new insights on the links between the internal structure of firms, their incentives, and their performance.

The first two papers deal with labour-managed (LM) firms. While Okuguchi and Szidarovszky investigate the existence of equilibrium in a Cournot oligopoly with LM firms using Brouwer's fixed point theorem, Ohnishi studies the possibility of using wage premia in LM markets.

In the third paper, Gianpaolo Rossini investigates the plausibility of price-setting behaviour in a model where the firms must choose between vertical integration and outsourcing under uncertainty. He examines two different vertical relationships, namely a non symmetric (imperfectly) competitive one and a cooperative one based on a bargaining process among vertical production stages (or firms). In the first, quantity setting is preferred by firms, because it eliminates uncertainty in expected terms. In the second, he shows that uncertainty entails an asymmetric distribution of gains along the vertical production chain.

The fourth paper deals with fair trade, which is, so to speak, a new entry in the current spectrum of strategies a firm could adopt. Here, Becchetti and Gianfreda show that a desirable side-effect generated by the introduction of socially responsible goods is that of inducing socially responsible imitation by traditional profit maximizing firms. As a consequence, there arises a consumer-driven market mechanism promoting equity.

The papers by Dragone and Cellini and Lambertini revisit

Vickers's (1985) model of strategic delegation to tackle, respectively, the issues of (i) horizontal mergers and collusion, and (ii) outsourcing. Dragone shows that, in a Cournot oligopoly, the presence of a managerial fringe may indeed affect the stability of collusion in outputs. The interesting policy implication of his analysis is that, choosing the appropriate size of the fringe, a regulator may affect the equilibrium outcome so as to enhance social welfare. Cellini and Lambertini analyse the make-or-buy decisions of firms in a mixed duopoly where one unit is a pure profit-seeker while the other has operated a strategic separation between ownership and control. The main finding is that that different equilibria may arise, depending on demand and cost parameters: if the technology employed for producing the intermediate input is too costly, then the internal organization of firms at equilibrium is mixed, implying a conflict between private and social preferences, as the latter would always prefer vertical integration to outsourcing.

The last three papers deal with the empirical side of the issue, that is, they focus on the measurement of firms' performance. Oropallo and Rossetti use micro-data drawn from Istat structural business statistics on Italian firms to evaluate the impact of several factors, such as investments, human capital, service inputs, age, and context variables, on profits and productivity.

Casaburi, Gattai and Minerva look at the empirical evidence about the link between firms' performance and their international status, using a sample of Italian enterprises. Their results can be summarized as follows: (i) firms that engage in the foreign production of final goods, in addition to export activities, are more productive than firms that only export abroad; (ii) firms that engage in final goods off-shoring are more productive than firms that engage in inputs off-shoring; and (iii) over the period 1998-2003, exporters' performance in Italy was not any better than non-exporters' one. The authors' overall appraisal of the analysis carried out in their paper is that the better performance characterising globally engaged firms can be mainly attributed to the selection driven by fixed costs associated to operating internationally. Breda, Cappariello and Zizza use input-output tables to estimate the import content of exports for several European countries, interpreting it as a measure of

5

internationalisation in recent years. They show that Italy experienced the weakest growth whereas Germany enjoyed the most sizeable rise, and argue that Italian firms might have felt a lower pressure to transform their organisation as a result of lagged effects of the Lira crisis in the first half of the '90s.

BIBLIOGRAPHY

AOKI M., *The Co-operative Game Theory of the Firm*, Oxford, Clarendon Press, 1984.

BAUMOL W., «On the Theory of Oligopoly», *Economica*, no. 25, 1958, pages 187-198.

FERSHTMAN C. - JUDD K., «Equilibrium Incentives in Oligopoly», *American Economic Review*, no. 77, 1987, pages 927-940.

GROSSMAN G.M. - HELPMAN E., «Integration versus Outsourcing in Industry Equilibrium», *Quarterly Journal of Economics*, no. 117, 2002, pages 85-120.

IRELAND N. - LAW P., *The Economics of Labor Managed Enterprises*, London, Croom Helm, 1982.

MARRIS R., «A Model of Managerial Enterprise», *Quarterly Journal of Economics*, no. 77, 1963, pages 185-209.

MCLAREN J., «Globalization and Vertical Structure», *American Economic Review*, no. 90, 2000, pages 1239-1254.

PENROSE E., *The Theory of the Growth of the Firm*, Oxford, Blackwell, 1959.

SERTEL M., *Workers and Incentives*, Amsterdam, North Holland, 1982.

SOLOW R., «Some Implications of Alternative Criteria for the Firm», in MARRIS R. - WOOD A. (eds.), *The Corporate Economy*, London, Macmillan, 1971.

VANEK J., *The General Theory of Labor-managed Market Economies*, Ithaca (NY), Cornell University Press, 1977.

VICKERS J., «Delegation and the Theory of the Firm», *Economic Journal*, no. 95 (Conference Papers), 1985, pages 138-47.

WARD N., «The Firm in Illyria: Market Syndicalism», *American Economic Review*, no. 48, 1958, pages 566-589.

WILLIAMSON O., «Profit, Growth and Sales Maximisation», *Economica*, no. 33, 1966, pages 1-16.

Existence and Uniqueness
of Equilibrium in Labor-Managed
Cournot Oligopoly

Koji Okuguchi - **Ferenc Szidarovszky***

Gifu Shotoku Gakuen University   University of Arizona

Labor-managed Cournot oligopoly with or without product differentiation is analyzed. First, the existence of Cournot equilibrium which is not necessarily unique is proved under general conditions based on the Brouwer fixed point theorem, which does not provide a direct computer method for finding the equilibrium. Second, a constructive proof of finding the unique equilibrium is presented for Cournot labor-managed oligopoly without product differentiation.
[JEL Classification: L13, P13]

1. - Introduction

Ward (1958) has first shown perverse behavior of a competitive labor-managed firm whose objective is maximization of dividends per unit of labor in the firm. Hill and Waterson (1983) and Neary (1984) have analyzed labor-managed Cournot oligopoly without product differentiation. Okuguchi (1986) and Sertel (1991, 1993) have introduced product differentiation into labor-managed oligopoly. Okuguchi (1986) has proved that under a set of conditions, the price-adjusting Bertrand oligopoly equilibrium prices are not higher than the quantity-adjusting Cournot oligopoly equilibrium prices in labor-managed oligopoly with product differentiation. Okuguchi (1992) has also provided existence and stability proof of equilibrium in labor-managed

---

* <*okuguchi@gifu.shotoku.ac.jp*>; <*szidar@sie.arizona.edu*>.

quantity-adjusting Cournot oligopoly based on the contraction mapping theorem.

In this paper we will examine the existence and uniqueness of Cournot equilibrium in labor-managed oligopoly, first with and then without product differentiation. We will prove the existence of equilibrium under more general conditions than those in earlier works. In this proof we will use the Brouwer fixed point theorem, so the proof does not provide computer method to find the equilibrium. We will next prove an existence and uniqueness of equilibrium under more restrictive conditions basing on the idea of Szidarovszky and Yakowitz (1977), where the responses of the firms are functions of the industry output. This paper proceeds as follows. In Section 2 the existence theorem will be proved for labor-managed (LM for short) Cournot oligopoly with product differentiation. We will note that this theorem ensures the existence of equilibrium in LM Cournot oligopoly without product differentiation. In Section 3 a constructive proof of the existence and uniqueness of the equilibrium will be given, providing a practical method to compute the equilibrium. Section 4 concludes the paper.

2. - LM Cournot Oligopoly with Product Differentiation

Let $x_i = g_i(l_i)$, $g_i(0) = 0$ be the production function of firm i in LM Cournot oligopoly with n firms and with product differentiation, where x_i and l_i are firm i's output and labor, respectively. Let $p_i = f^i(x_1, x_2, ..., x_n)$ be the firm's inverse demand function. We assume that g_i and f^i are twice continuously differentiable for all i. Further we assume for all i and $j \neq i$:

(A) $$g_i' > 0, g_i'' \leq 0$$

(B) $$f_i^i = \frac{\partial f^i}{\partial x_i} < 0, f_j^i = \frac{\partial f^i}{\partial x_j} \leq 0$$

The second inequality in (B) implies that any two products

are either substitutes or independent of each other. We will return to the case of complement goods in a future paper. If k_i denotes firm i's fixed cost, then its dividends per unit labor is given as

(1)
$$v_i = \frac{g_i(l_i)f^i(g_1(l_1),...,g_n(l_n)) - k_i}{l_i}$$

In the following analysis we assume un upper bound L_i for l_i, i.e., $l_i \in [0, L_i]$. This assumption is plausible, since firms have capacity limits for their outputs, and as was observed in former socialistic economies, an increase in already large l_i does not bring forth further output. In the latter case it is easy to see that the best response of each firm has to be below this threshold.

By simple differentiation we have

(2)
$$\frac{\partial v_i}{\partial l_i} = \frac{u_i}{l_i^2}$$

(3)
$$u_i = (g_i' f^i + g_i f_i^i g_i') l_i - (g_i f^i - k_i)$$

Assume that for all i

(C)
$$f^i + g_i f_i^i > 0, \quad f_i^i + g_i f_{ii}^i < 0$$

We then have

(4)
$$\frac{\partial u_i}{\partial l_i} = g_i''(f^i + g_i f_i^i) + (g_i')^2(2f_i^i + g_i f_{ii}^i)l_i < 0$$

The best response of firm i is as follows

(5)
$$R_i(l_{-i}) = \begin{cases} L_i, u_i(L_i, l_{-i}) \geq 0 \\ l_i^*, u_i(L_i, l_{-i}) < 0 \end{cases}$$

where $l_{-i} = (l_1, ..., l_{i-1}, l_{i+1}, ..., l_n)$, and l_i^* is the unique positive solution of the monotonic equation

(6)
$$u_i(l_i, l_{-i}) = 0$$

Note that at $l_i = 0$, $u_i(0, l_{-i}) > 0$. In the second case of (5)

since u_i is strictly decreasing in l_i by *(4)*, the implicit function theorem implies that $R_i(l_{-i})$ is continuous. If we consider it as formally a function of vector $l = (l_i, ..., l_n)$, then the mapping R $(l) = (R_1(l), ..., R_n(l))$ maps a compact, convex set $[0, L_1] \times ... \times [0, L_n]$ into itself. Therefore it has at least one fixed point by the Brouwer fixed point theorem. Hence the following existence theorem.

THEOREM 1: Assume *(A)*, *(B)* and *(C)* hold. Then there exists at least one equilibrium in *LM* Cournot oligopoly with product differentiation.

In the case of no product differentiation, v_i reads

(7)
$$v_i = \frac{g_i(l_i)f(g_1(l_1) + ... + g_n(l_n)) - k_i}{l_i}$$

where *f* is the inverse market demand function for a homogeneous goods. In this case *(B)* and *(C)* above become

(B')
$$f' < 0$$

(C')
$$f + g_i f' > 0, \; f' + g_i f'' < 0$$

respectively. The first inequality implies that firm *i*'s marginal revenue is positive and the second one that it is strictly decreasing in its output.

3. - LM Cournot Oligopoly without Product Differentiation

In this section we will be concerned with the uniqueness of the equilibrium in the absence of product differentiation. Let $s = g_1(l_1) + ... + g_n(l_n)$ be the industry output for the homogeneous goods. Then

(8)
$$v_i = \frac{g_i(l_i')f(s - g_i(l_i) + g_i(l_i')) - k_i}{l_i}$$

where we assume firm i changes its labor input from l_i to l'_i. Clearly $l'_i = l_i$ is the payoff maximizing if either

$$l_i = L_i \text{ and } \frac{\partial v_i}{\partial l'_i} \geq 0, \forall l'_i$$

or

$$l_i < L_i \text{ and } \frac{\partial v_i}{\partial l'_i} \begin{cases} \geq 0, \forall l'_i < l_i \\ \leq 0, \forall l'_i > l_i \end{cases}$$

Note that equation *(2)* holds with u_i replaced with u'_i defined by

(9) $\quad u'_i(l_i, s) = (g'_i(l_i) f(s) + g_i(l_i) f'(s) g'_i(l_i)) l_i - (g_i(l_i) f(s) - k_i)$

and the best response of firm i as a function of s can be expressed as follows.

(10) $$\Phi_i(s) = \begin{cases} L_i, u'_i(L_i, s) \geq 0 \\ l^*_i, \text{ otherwise,} \end{cases}$$

where l^*_i is the unique solution of equation

(11) $\quad u'_i(l_i, s) = (g'_i(l_i)f(s) + g_i(l_i)f'(s)g'_i(l_i))l_i - (g_i(l_i)f(s) - k_i) = 0$

At $l_i = 0$, the left hand side is positive, and at $l_i = L_i$, it is negative since the second case of *(10)* applies. Given s, the derivative of the left hand side with respect to change in l_i is

(12) $\quad \dfrac{\partial \pi_i}{\partial l_i} = g''_i(l_i)l_i(f(s) + g_i(l_i)f'(s)) + (g'_i)^2 f'(s) + g_i(l_i)g'_i(l_i)f'(s) < 0$

Hence $u'_i(l_i, s)$ is strictly decreasing in l_i. Therefore, the implicit function theorem implies that $\Phi_i(s)$ exists and is continuous in s. Consider finally the single variable equation

(13) $$\sum_{i=1}^{n} g_i(\Phi_i(s)) - s = 0$$

13

At $s = 0$, the left hand side is nonnegative, at

$$s = \sum_{i=1}^{n} g_i(L_i)$$

it is nonpositive. Therefore, there exists at least one solution, implying the existence of at least one Cournot equilibrium. Since functions $\Phi_i(s)$ and the solution of equation *(13)* can be easily obtained, we have a practical method for computing equilibria. The above derivation is a constructive proof of Theorem 1 for the case without product differentiation.

Next we will show that under an additional assumption, the equilibrium is unique. By simple differentiation

(14) $$\frac{\partial u_i'}{\partial s} = g_i'(l_i)l_i(f'(s) + g_i'(l_i)f''(s)) - g_i(l_i)f'(s)$$

. which has ambiguous sign. If we assume in addition to assumptions *(A)*, *(B')* and *(C')* for all i

(D) $$g_i'(f' + g_i'f'')\,l_i - g_if' < 0$$

then, we have $\partial u_i'/\partial s < 0$. The monotonicity of u_i' in l_i and s implies that $\Phi_i(s)$ is decreasing in s. If one or both values s and s' for which $s < s'$ holds are in the first case of *(10)*, then this is obvious. Otherwise, assume that $\Phi_i(s) \leq \Phi_i(s')$, then

$$0 = u_i'(\Phi_i(s), s) > u_i'(\Phi_i(s), s') \geq u_i'(\Phi_i(s'), s') = 0$$

which is a contradiction. Therefore the left hand side of *(13)* is strictly decreasing in s, hence equation *(13)* has a unique solution. Summarizing we have established

THEOREM 2. Under assumptions *(A)*, *(B')*, *(C')* and *(D)*, there exists a unique equilibrium in LM Cournot oligopoly without product differentiation.

A few words on assumption *(D)* may be in order. Since

14

(15) $$g_i'(f' + g_i f'')l_i - g_i f' = f' l_i (g_i' - \frac{g_i}{l_i}) + g_i'^2 f'' l_i$$

and $g_i' \le g_i/l_i$ by assumption *(A)*, the right hand side of *(15)* becomes positive if $f'' = 0$, violating the assumption (D). However, if f'' is negative with sufficiently large absolute value, *(15)* may become negative. Next, define two elasticities and market share for firm i as

$$\varepsilon_i \equiv \frac{g_i' l_i}{g_i} > 0, \eta_i \equiv \frac{f'' s}{f'}, \omega_i \equiv \frac{x_i}{s}$$

Then assumption *(D)* reads

(16) $$\frac{1}{\varepsilon_i} - \eta_i \omega_i < 1$$

4. - Conclusion

In this paper we have given a proof of the existence of equilibrium in LM Cournot oligopoly with product differentiation based on the Brouwer fixed point theorem. The proof guarantees only the existence of at least one equilibrium, and does not provide computer method to find the equilibrium. The uniqueness of the equilibrium and its stability property have been examined by Okuguchi (1992) under more restrictive conditions. Our existence proof can be directly applied to LM Cournot oligopoly without product differentiation. Under an additional assumption the uniqueness of the equilibrium is guaranteed and a practical method could be developed for the computation of the equilibrium.

BIBLIOGRAPHY

Bonin J.P. - Putterman L., *Economics of Cooperation and the Labor-Managed Economy*, London - New York, Harwood Academic Publishers, 1987.

Hill M. - Waterson M., «Labor-Managed Cournot Oligopoly and Industry Output», *Journal of Comparative Economics*, vol. 7, 1983, pages 43-52.

Ireland N.J. - Law P.J., *The Economics of Labour-Managed Enterprises*, London, Croom Helm, 1982.

Neary H.M., «Labor-Managed Cournot Oligopoly and Industry Output: Comment», *Journal of Comparative Economics*, vol. 8, 1984, pages 322-327.

Okuguchi K., «Labor-Managed Bertrand and Cournot Oligopolies», *Journal of Economics*, vol. 46, 1986, pages 115-122.

— —, «Labor-Managed Cournot Oligopoly with Product Differentiation», *Journal of Economics*, vol. 56, 1992, pages 197-208.

Sertel M.R., «Workers' Enterprises in Imperfect Competition», *Journal of Comparative Economics*, vol. 15, 1991, pages 698-710.

— —, «Workers' Enterprises in Price Competition», *Managerial and Decision Economics*, vol. 14, 1993, pages 445-449.

Szidarovszky F. - Yakowitz S., «A New Proof of the Existence and Uniqueness of the Cournot Equilibrium», *International Economic Review*, vol. 18, 1977, pages 787-790.

Ward B., «The Firm in Illyria: Market Syndicalism», *American Economic Review*, vol. 48, 1958, pages 566-589.

Wage-Rise Contract
and Cournot Competition
with Labor-Managed Firms

Kazuhiro Ohnishi*

Osaka University and Institute for Basic Economic Science

This paper examines the effectiveness of the wage-rise-contract policy as a strategic commitment in a two-stage quantity-setting model with two labor-managed income-per-worker-maximizing firms. The policy is a promise by the firm that it will announce a certain output level and a wage premium rate, and if it actually produces more than the announced output level, then it will pay each employee a wage premium uniformly. In the first stage, each firm independently decides whether or not to adopt the policy. In the second stage, each firm independently chooses its actual output. It is then shown that there exists an equilibrium in which at least one firm adopts the policy. [JEL Classification: C72; D21; L20]

1. - Introduction

The pioneering work on a theoretical model of a labor-managed firm was conducted by Ward (1958). Thereafter, many economists have studied the behaviors of labor-managed firms.[1] Laffont and Moreaux (1985) examine the welfare properties of free entry Cournot equilibria in labor-managed economies and show that Cournot equilibria are efficient provided that the market is sufficiently large.[2] Zhang (1993) and Haruna (1996)

---

* <ohnishi@e.people.or.jp>.
[1] See IRELAND N.J. - LAW P.J. (1982); STEPHAN F.H. (1982) and BONIN J.P. - PUTTERMAN L. (1987) for excellent surveys.
[2] For free entry models, see also HILL M. - WATERSON M. (1983) and KAMSHAD K.M. (1997).

17

apply a Dixit (1980), Bulow *et* al. (1985) framework of entry deterrence to a labor-managed industry and show that a labor-managed incumbent firm has a greater incentive to hold excess capacity to deter entry than a corresponding profit-maximizing incumbent firm. Okuguchi (1993) examines two models of duopoly with product differentiation and with only labor-managed firms, in one of which two firms' strategies are outputs (labor-managed Cournot duopoly) and prices become strategic variables in the other (labor-managed Bertrand duopoly). He shows that reaction functions are upward-sloping under general conditions in both labor-managed Bertrand and Cournot duopolies with product differentiation.[3] Lambertini and Rossini (1998) analyze the behavior of labor-managed firms in a two-stage Cournot duopoly model with capital strategic interaction and show that labor-managed firms choose their capital commitments according to the level of interest rate, unlike what usually happens when only profit-maximizing firms operate in the market. Lambertini (2001) examines a spatial differentiation duopoly model and shows that if both firms are labor-managed, there exists a (symmetric) subgame perfect equilibrium in pure strategies with firms located at the first and third quartiles, if and only if the setup cost is low enough. Drago and Turnbull (1992) provide a model of work effort and wage incentives in the worker-owned or labor-managed firm and show that if employee-owners can establish binding effort matching agreements, purely collective incentives are optimal. There are many excellent further studies exploring other extensions, such as R&D investments and intraindustry trade.

We use a two-stage quantity-setting model in which two labor-managed income-per-worker-maximizing firms compete. We consider the wage-rise-contract policy (henceforth WRCP) as a strategic commitment.[4] WRCP is a promise by the firm that it will announce a certain output level and a wage premium rate, and if

---

[3] See also DELBONO F. - ROSSINI G. (1992); FUTAGAMI K. - OKAMURA M. (1996) and LAMBERTINI L. - ROSSINI G. (1998).

[4] For details see OHNISHI K. (2003).

it actually produces more than the announced output level, then it will pay each employee a wage premium uniformly. We consider the following situation. In the first stage, each firm independently decides whether or not to adopt WRCP. At the end of the first stage, each firm knows the rival's behavior in the first stage. In the second stage, each firm independently chooses and sells its actual output. In this model, we find that there exists an equilibrium in which at least one firm adopts WRCP.

The purpose of this paper is to show the effectiveness of WRCP in the two-stage quantity-setting model with two labor-managed income-per-worker-maximizing firms.

The paper is organized as follows. In Section 2, we formulate the model. Section 3 gives supplementary explanations of the model. Section 4 discusses the equilibrium of the model. Section 5 concludes the paper. Finally, the Appendix provides formal proofs.

2. - The Model

Let us consider a market with two labor-managed income-per-worker-maximizing firms, firm 1 and firm 2. For the remainder of this paper, when i and j are used to refer to firms in an expression, they should be understood to refer to 1 and 2 with $i \neq j$. The market price is determined by the inverse demand function $p(Q)$, where $Q = \sum_{i=1}^{2} q_i$ denotes the aggregate quantity. We assume that $p' < 0$ and $p'' \leq 0$. The market will be modelled by means of the following two-stage game. In the first stage, each firm independently decides whether or not to adopt WRCP. If firm i adopts WRCP, then it chooses an output level $q_i^* \geq 0$ and a wage premium rate $t_i > 0$. Furthermore, firm i agrees to pay each employee a wage premium uniformly if it actually produces more than q_i^*. At the end of the first stage, each firm knows the rival's behavior in the first stage. In the second stage, each firm independently chooses and sells its actual output $q_i > 0$.

Therefore, firm i's income per worker is given by

(1)
$$
V_i = \begin{cases}
\dfrac{p(Q)q_i - m_iq_i - f_i}{l_i(q_i)} & \text{if } q_i \leq q_i^* \\[3mm]
\dfrac{p(Q)q_i - m_iq_i - (q_i - q_i^*)t_i - f_i}{l_i(q_i)} & \text{if } q_i \geq q_i^*
\end{cases}
$$

where $m_i > 0$ denotes firm i's total cost for each unit of output, $f_i > 0$ firm i's fixed cost, and $l_i(q_i)$ the number of workers in firm i. We assume that $l_i' > 0$ and $l_i'' > 0$. These are standard assumptions. In this paper, we will discuss the pure-strategy subgame-perfect Nash equilibrium by backward induction.

3. - Reaction Functions

We derive the reaction functions in quantities.[5] The equilibrium occurs where each firm maximizes its objective with respect to its own output level, given the output level of its rival. Firm i's reaction function when the marginal cost is constantly equal to m_i is defined by

(2)
$$
R_i(q_j) = \arg\max_{q_i} \left[\frac{p(Q)q_i - m_iq_i - f_i}{l_i(q_i)} \right]
$$

and firm i's reaction function when the marginal cost is constantly equal to $m_i + t_i$ is defined by

(3)
$$
R_i^t(q_j) = \arg\max_{q_i} \left[\frac{p(Q)q_i - (m_i + t_i)q_i + t_iq_i^* - f_i}{l_i(q_i)} \right]
$$

Therefore, if firm i adopts WRCP, then its best response is as follows:

(4)
$$
R_i^W(q_j) = \begin{cases}
R_i(q_j) & \text{if } q_i < q_i^* \\
q_i^* & \text{if } q_i = q_i^* \\
R_i^t(q_j) & \text{if } q_i > q_i^*
\end{cases}
$$

---

[5] For the reaction functions of labor-manage firms, see DELBONO F. - ROSSINI G. (1992); OKUGUCHI K. (1993); FUTAGAMI K. - OKAMURA M. (1996) and LAMBERTINI L. - ROSSINI G. (1998).

Firm i aims to maximize its income per worker with respect to its own output level, given the output level of firm j. The equilibrium must satisfy the following conditions: The first-order condition for firm i when the marginal cost for output is constantly equal to m_i is

$$(5) \qquad (p'q_i + p - m_i)\, l_i - (pq_i - m_i q_i - f_i)\, l'_i = 0$$

the first-order condition for firm i when the marginal cost is constantly equal to $m_i + t_i$ is

$$(6) \qquad (p'q_i + p - m_i - t_i)\, l_i - (pq_i - m_i q_i - t_i q_i + t_i q_i^* - f_i)\, l'_i = 0$$

the second-order condition for firm i when the marginal cost for output is constantly equal to m_i is

$$(7) \qquad (p''q_i + 2p')\, l_i - (pq_i - m_i q_i - f_i)\, l''_i < 0$$

and the second-order condition for firm i when the marginal cost is constantly equal to $m_i + t_i$ is

$$(8) \qquad (p''q_i + 2p')\, l_i - (pq_i - m_i q_i - t_i q_i + t_i q_i^* - f_i)\, l''_i < 0$$

Furthermore, we have

$$(9) \qquad R'_i(q_j) = -\frac{p''q_i l_i + p'(l_i - q_i l'_i)}{(p''q_i + 2p')l_i - (pq_i - m_i q_i - f_i)l''_i}$$

and

$$(10) \qquad R^{t'}_i(q_j) = -\frac{p''q_i l_i + p'(l_i - q_i l'_i)}{(p''q_i + 2p')l_i - (pq_i - m_i q_i - t_i q_i + t_i q_i^* - f_i)l''_i}$$

Since $l''_i > 0$, $l_i - q_i l'_i < 0$, so $p''q_i l_i + p'(l_i - q_i l'_i)$ is positive. The following result is implied:

LEMMA 1. Under Cournot competition, both $R_i(q_j)$ and $R^t_i(q_j)$ are upward sloping.

Both firms' reaction curves are drawn in Graph 1. R_i is firm

GRAPH 1

REACTION CURVES IN QUANTITY SPACE

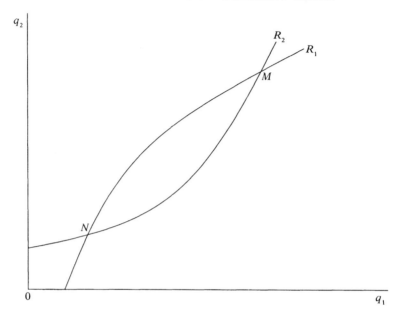

i's reaction curve when the marginal cost for output is constantly equal to m_i. Both firms' reaction curves are upward sloping. This means that both firms treat quantities as strategic complements. The reaction curves cross twice. Only point N is a stable Cournot equilibrium, since in point M firm 2's reaction curve crosses firm 1's from above.[6] In this paper, we will discuss only stable Cournot equilibria.

4. - Results

First, consider the case in which only firm 1 can adopt WRCP. When only firm 2 adopts WRCP, a symmetric discussion applies. Firm 1 aims to maximize its income per worker. Therefore, it is

---

[6] See LAMBERTINI L. - ROSSINI G. (1998).

thought that firm 1 will adopt WRCP if its income per worker increases by doing so, while firm 1 will not adopt WRCP if its income per worker decreases by doing so. The unilateral case of the model runs as follows. In the first stage, firm 1 decides whether or not to adopt WRCP. If firm 1 adopts WRCP, then it chooses an output level q_1^* and a wage premium rate t_1. Furthermore, firm 1 agrees to pay each employee a wage premium uniformly if it actually produces more than q_1^*. On the other hand, firm 2 does not adopt WRCP. In the second stage, each firm independently chooses its actual output q_i.

We briefly discuss the equilibrium of the unilateral case by using Graph 2. R_1^t is firm 1's reaction curve when the marginal cost for output is constantly equal to $m_1 + t_1$. If firm 1 adopts WRCP, its marginal cost increases and thus its reaction curve shifts to the left. The equilibrium is decided in a Cournot fashion,

GRAPH 2

THE UNILATERAL CASE

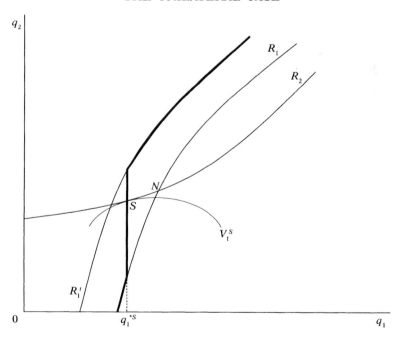

i.e. the intersection of both firms' reaction curves gives us a stable equilibrium. Therefore, firm 1's unilateral equilibrium can occur at the appropriate point at and to the left of N on R_2. If firm 1 chooses q_1^{*S} and t_1^S and offers WRCP, then from *(4)*, its reaction curve becomes the kinked bold lines drawn in Graph 2. On the other hand, since firm 2 cannot adopt WRCP, its reaction curve is R_2. Hence, firm 1's unilateral equilibrium occurs at S. If neither firm adopts WRCP, then the equilibrium occurs at N.

Now, we can state the following proposition:

PROPOSITION 1. Suppose that only firm 1 can adopt WRCP. Then there exists an equilibrium which coincides with the Stackelberg solution where firm 1 is the leader and firm 2 is the follower. At equilibrium, each firm's income per worker is higher than in the Cournot equilibrium with no WRCP.

Proposition 1 means that offering WRCP enables a firm to act as a Stackelberg leader. Thus, the best firm i can do is to adopt WRCP if firm j does not adopt WRCP.

Next, consider the case in which both firms can adopt WRCP. Proposition 1 states that, when one firm unilaterally adopts WRCP, there is an equilibrium which coincides with the Stackelberg outcome. By symmetry, there are two such equilibria. Furthermore, if each firm's income per worker is higher when both firms adopt WRCP than when one firm unilaterally adopts WRCP, then there is an equilibrium in which both firms will adopt WRCP.

We briefly discuss the equilibrium by using Graph 3. R_i^t is firm i's reaction curve when the marginal cost for output is constantly equal to $m_i + t_i$. If firm 1 chooses and q_1^{*E} and t_1^E and adopts WRCP, then firm 1's reaction curve becomes the kinked bold lines. Furthermore, if firm 2 chooses q_2^{*E} and t_2^E and adopts WRCP, then firm 2's reaction curve becomes the kinked bold broken lines. Therefore, the intersection of their reaction curves becomes a point like E as drawn in Graph 3. Proposition 1 states that if one firm adopts WRCP, each firm's income per worker is higher than in the Cournot equilibrium with no WRCP. This ensures that at least one firm will adopt WRCP in equilibrium.

24

GRAPH 3

THE BILATERAL CASE

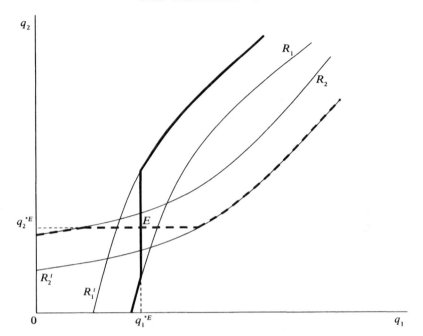

The main result of this study is described by the following proposition:

PROPOSITION 2. There exists an equilibrium in which at least one firm adopts WRCP. At equilibrium, each firm's income per worker is higher than in the Cournot equilibrium with no WRCP.

Proposition 2 means that WRCP enables both firms to earn more in a noncooperative setting, *i.e.* it facilitates tacit collusion.

5. - Conclusion

We have examined the effectiveness of WRCP in a two-stage Cournot model with two labor-managed income-per-worker-maximizing firms. First, we have shown that if one firm unilaterally adopts WRCP, then there exists an equilibrium which coincides with the Stackelberg solution where the adopting firm is the leader, and at equilibrium each firm's income per worker is higher than in the Cournot equilibrium with no WRCP. Second, we have examined the case in which both firms can adopt WRCP. We have then shown that there exists an equilibrium in which at least one firm adopts WRCP, and at equilibrium each firm's income per worker is higher than in the Cournot equilibrium with no WRCP. Since WRCP enables both firms to earn more in a noncooperative setting, the results indicate that WRCP facilitates tacit collusion. As a consequence, it is shown that WRCP is an effective policy.

9

APPENDIX

First of all, we will present the next two supplementary lemmas.

LEMMA 2. If firm i adopts WRCP, then in equilibrium $q_i = q_i^*$.

PROOF. First, consider the possibility that $q_i > q_i^*$ in equilibrium. From *(1)*, firm i's income-per-worker is

$$V_i = \frac{p(Q)q_i - m_i q_i - (q_i - q_i^*)t_i - f_i}{l_i(q_i)}$$

Here, firm i can increase its income per worker by increasing q_i^*, and the equilibrium point does not change in $q_i \geq q_i^*$. Hence, $q_i > q_i^*$ does not result in an equilibrium.

Next, consider the possibility that $q_i < q_i^*$ in equilibrium. From *(1)*, we see that firm i's marginal cost is m_i. It is impossible for firm i to change its output in equilibrium because such a strategy is not credible. That is, WRCP does not function as a strategic commitment. Q.E.D.

LEMMA 3. Firm i's optimal output is smaller when it adopts WRCP than when it does not.

PROOF. From *(1)*, we see that WRCP will never decrease the marginal cost of firm i. The first-order condition for firm i when its marginal cost is m_i is *(5)*, and the first-order condition for firm i when its marginal cost is $m_i + t_i$ is *(6)*. Here, t_i is positive. Lemma 2 shows that firm i's optimal output when it adopts WRCP coincides with q_i^*. To satisfy *(6)*, $(p'q_i + p - m_i)\,l_i - (pq_i - m_i q_i - f_i)\,l_i'$ must be positive. Thus, firm i's income-per-worker-maximizing output is smaller when its marginal cost is $m_i + t_i$ than when its marginal cost is m_i. Q.E.D.

Now, we will prove the propositions.

PROOF of PROPOSITION 1

Firm 1's objective is to maximize its income per worker. The first-order condition for firm 1 when the marginal cost for output is constantly equal to m_1 is (5). We consider firm 1's Stackelberg leader output when each firm's marginal cost is constantly equal to m_i. Firm 1 selects q_1, and firm 2 selects q_2 after observing q_1. If firm 1 is the Stackelberg leader, then it maximizes its income per worker $V_1 (q_1, R_2 (q_1))$ with respect to q_1. Therefore, firm 1's Stackelberg leader output satisfies the first-order condition:

$$(11) \qquad (p'q_1 + p - m_1) \, l_1 - (pq_1 - m_1q_1 - f_1) \, l_1' + p'q_1R_2' = 0$$

From $p' < 0$ and $R_2' > 0$, to satisfy (11), $(p'q_1 + p - m_1) \, l_1 - (pq_1 - m_1q_1 - f_1) \, l_1'$ must be positive. Hence, firm 1's Stackelberg leader output is smaller than its Cournot output. Furthermore, $V_1 = (p(Q)q_1 - m_1q_1 - f_1)/l_1 (q_1)$ is continuous and concave on q_1. In R_2, firm 1's income per worker is the highest at its Stackelberg leader point, and the further the point on R_2 gets from firm 1's Stackelberg leader point, the more firm 1's income per worker decreases. Lemma 3 shows that firm 1's income-per-worker-maximizing output is smaller when it adopts WRCP than when it does not. From (6), we see that a decrease in firm 1's output is decided by the value of t_1. Let t_1 be a variable that can take any value more than zero. Thus, the equilibrium coincides with the Stackelberg solution where firm 1 is the leader and firm 2 is the follower.

In R_2, firm 1's income per worker is the highest at its Stackelberg leader point. Lemma 2 shows that $q_1 = q_1^*$ in equilibrium. Hence, firm 1's Stackelberg leader income per worker is higher than in the Cournot equilibrium with no WRCP. Firm 1's Stackelberg leader output is smaller than its Cournot output. Since $\partial V_2/\partial q_1 = p'q_2/l_2 < 0$, firm 2's Stackelberg follower income per worker is also higher than in the Cournot equilibrium with no WRCP. Q.E.D.

PROOF of PROPOSITION 2

In the first stage, each firm decides whether or not to adopt

WRCP. In the second stage, each firm chooses its actual output q_i independently, and each firm's income per worker is decided. Hence, we can consider the following matrix:

		Firm 2	
		WRCP	No WRCP
Firm 1	WRCP	V_1^E, V_2^E	V_1^L, V_2^F
	No WRCP	V_1^F, V_2^L	V_1^N, V_2^N

From Proposition 1, we see that $V_i^F, V_i^L > V_i^N$. Hence, there is an equilibrium in which someone adopts WRCP. Therefore, if $V_i^F > V_i^E$, then (No WRCP, WRCP) and (WRCP, No WRCP) are both equilibria. From Proposition 1, we see that the rest of Proposition 2 hold if one firm unilaterally adopts WRCP. On the other hand, if (WRCP, WRCP) is an equilibrium, then $V_i^E \geq V_i^F (> V_i^N)$. Q.E.D.

BIBLIOGRAPHY

BONIN J.P. - PUTTERMAN L., *Economics of Cooperation and the Labor-manage Economy*, New York, Harwood Academic Publisher, 1987.

BULOW J. - GEANAKOPLOS J. - KLEMPERER P., «Holding Idle Capacity to Deter Entry», *Economic Journal*, vol. 95, 1985, pages 178-182.

COOPER T.E., «Most-favored-customer Pricing and Tacit Collusion», *Rand Journal of Economics*, vol. 17, 1986, pages 377-388.

DELBONO F. - ROSSINI G., «Competition Policy vs Horizontal Merger with Public Entrepreneurial, and Labor-managed Firms», *Journal of Comparative Economics*, vol. 16, 1992, pages 226-240.

DIXIT A.K., «The Role of Investment in Entry-deterrence», *Economic Journal*, vol. 90, 1980, pages 95-106.

DRAGO R. - TURNBULL G.K., «Wage Incentives in Labour-managed and Profit Maximizing firms», *Australian Economic Papers*, vol. 31, 1992, pages 311-324.

FUTAGAMI K. - OKAMURA M., «Strategic Investment: The Labor-managed Firm and the Profit-maximizing Firm», *Journal of Comparative Economics*, vol. 23, 1996, pages 73-91.

HARUNA S., «A Note on Holding Excess Capacity to Deter Entry in a Labour-managed Industry», *Canadian Journal of Economics*, vol. 29, 1996, pages 493-499.

HILL M. - WATERSON M., «Labor-managed Cournot Oligopoly and Industry Output», *Journal of Comparative Economics*, vol. 7, 1983, pages 43-51.

IRELAND N.J. - LAW P.J., *The Economics of Labor-managed Enterprises*, New York, St. Martin's Press, 1982.

KAMSHAD K.M., «A Model of the Free-entry Producer Cooperative», *Annals of Public and Cooperative Economics*, vol. 68, 1997, pages 225-245.

LAFFONT J.J. - MOREAUX M., «Large-market Cournot Equilibria in Labour-managed Economies», *Economica*, vol. 52, 1985, pages 153-165.

LAMBERTINI L., «Spatial Competition with Profit-maximising and Labour-managed Firms», *Papers in Regional Science*, vol. 80, 2001, pages 499-507.

LAMBERTINI L. - ROSSINI G., «Capital Commitment and Cournot Competition with Labour-managed and Profit-maximising Firms», *Australian Economic Papers*, vol. 37, 1998, pages 14-21.

NEARY H.M., «Labor-managed Cournot Oligopoly and Industry Output: A Comment, *Journal of Comparative Economics*, vol. 8, 1984, pages 322-327.

— —, «Comparative Statics of the Ward-Domar LMF: A Profit Function Approach», *Journal of Comparative Economics*, vol. 12, 1988, pages 159-181.

NEILSON W.S. - WINTER H., «Unilateral Most-favored-customer Pricing: A Comparison with Stackelberg», *Economics Letters*, vol. 38, 1992, pages 229-232.

OHNISHI K., «A Model of a Price-setting Duopoly with a Wage-rise Contract», *Australian Economic Papers*, vol. 42, 2003, pages 149-157.

— —, «A Mixed Duopoly with a Lifetime Employment Contract as a Strategic Commitment», *FinanzArchiv*, vol. 62, 2006, pages 108-123.

OKUGUCHI K., «Follower's Advantage in Labor-managed Duopoly», *Keio Economic Studies*, vol. 30, 1993, pages 1-5.

SERTEL M.R., «Workers' Enterprises in Imperfect Competition», *Journal of comparative Economics*, vol. 15, 1991, pages 698-710.

STEPHAN F.H. (ed.), *The Performance of Labour-managed Firms*, London, Macmillan Press, 1982.

STEWART G., «Strategic Entry Interactions Involving Profit-maximising and Labour-managed Firms», *Oxford Economic Papers*, vol. 43, 1991, pages 570-583.

VANEK J., *The General Theory of Labor-managed Market Economies*, Ithaca (NY), Cornell University Press, 1977.

WARD N., «The Firm in Illyria: Market Syndicalism», *American Economic Review*, vol. 48, 1958, pages 566-589.

ZHANG J., «Holding Excess Capacity to Deter Entry in a Labour-managed Industry», *Canadian Journal of Economics*, vol. 26, 1993, pages 222-234.

Price Setting is Popular among Firms: Will It Persist in Vertical Relationships with Market Uncertainty?

Gianpaolo Rossini*

University of Bologna

Price setting is popular among firms selling to consumers driven in their buying decisions mostly by price signals since they take for granted availability of goods. Is this enterprise behaviour justified when production is vertically organized along several stages? We consider two different market strategies, price setting and quantity setting and two different vertical relationships: a non symmetric (imperfectly) competitive one and a cooperative one based on a bargaining among vertical sections of production. In the first scenario, with certainty, price and quantity settings are alike, while with uncertainty quantity setting is preferred by firms. With bargaining and quantity setting, uncertainty leads to an asymmetric distribution of gains along the vertical chain of production. [JEL Classification: L1]

1. - Introduction

Most enterprises advertise their products communicating prices. Consumers are almost certain that they will be able to get the chosen good at the quoted price. This is common practice for both durable and nondurable goods markets. Price setting is

---

* *<gianpaolo.rossini@unibo.it>*, Department of Economics. The Author thanks Luca Lambertini for his comments and suggestions, while taking full responsibility for the content of this chapter. Moreover, the Author gratefully acknowledges the financial support of the University of Bologna under the 60% scheme for the a.y. 2006-7 and the financial support of the Italian Ministry of Education within the 40% scheme for the a.y. 2006-7.

popular among firms with the ability of adjusting supply without incurring substantial cost changes. Most production processes are organized along more than one vertical stage which may take place within the same firm (vertical integration) or in many separate enterprises (vertical disintegration or outsourcing). Since we do not know whether and to what extent the vertical organization affects marketing policies, it is worth investigating the relationship between vertical arrangements of production and price/quantity setting.

Vertical integration (VI) and its contrary, *i.e.*, outsourcing[1] (OS), have become quite hot issues in theoretical and applied literature (Acemoglu, Aghion, Griffith and Zilibotti, 2005; Acemoglu, Johnson and Mitton, 2005; Antràs and Helpman, 2004; Grossman and Helpman, 2002; Rossini, 2005, 2007; Rossini and Ricciardi, 2005), and also in policy discussions (Amiti and Wei, 2004).

The decision concerning which vertical arrangement to adopt, OS or VI, is a strategic choice that is affected by several externalities.

Two of them are worth mentioning.

The first externality concerns the act of going VI or OS. In a two stage vertical production process composed by a downstream (D) section manufacturing a final good and an upstream (U) section producing an intermediate input, whenever a U firm integrates with a D firm the market structure of the U production gets more concentrated. An opposite effect occurs if a VI enterprise splits into a U and a D firm. Changing the vertical arrangement gives rise to either a negative or a positive externality for rivals, altering the profitability of going OS or VI for subsequent firms (McLaren, 1999, 2000).

The second externality is dubbed "double marginalization" (Spengler, 1950; Williamson, 1971; Tirole, 1988; Perry, 1989): when the price of the final good increases, the profit of the U firm shrinks. This happens in all market structures but perfect competition. The aftermath of this is that VI turns out superior

---

[1] The definition of outsourcing used is not unanimously accepted. For a different taxonomy see BHAGWATI J. - PANAGARIYA A. - SRINIVASAN T.N. (2004).

from both a private and a social point of view, even though there are circumstances, related either to heterodox objectives of firms (Rossini, 2005), or to differentiation (Lambertini and Rossini, 2003; Pepall and Norman, 2001) or to market strategic substitutability (Buehler and Schmutzler, 2003) where this externality is weakened or even neutralized. The second externality arises when the vertical relationship between U and D mimics a Stackelberg duopoly, with U leader and D follower. The vertical asymmetry emerges since the final demand is faced by the D firm. For instance, if D produces motorbikes and U saddles, the demand for saddles is determined by the demand for motorbikes, not the other way round.

Empirically the question of private and social superiority of VI *vis à vis* OS has been analyzed by Slade (1998*a*, *b*) who casts doubts on some past stances of antitrust agencies.

Further externalities in vertical relationships are related to R&D and are theoretically investigated in Lambertini and Rossini (2008), Brocas (2003), Banerjee and Lin (2001), among others, while empirical studies date back to fundamental contributions of Teece (1976) and Armour and Teece (1981) all the way through more recent studies, such as Nemoto and Goto (2004) and Rossini and Ricciardi (2005). R&D vertical spillovers add a new source of external benefits in vertical arrangements and may interact with vertical restraints in a trade environment making sometimes VD superior (Rossini, 2007).

A way out of the second set of external effects comes from the cooperative approach, where U and D bargain over the price or the quantity of the input to be exchanged among them, as modelled in a Nash-Rubinstein Bargaining Solution (NBS) (Nash, 1950) or in one of its many refinements[2].

The adoption of a cooperative approach is a matter of judgement. The Stackelberg solution introduces a vertical asymmetry and is affected by an externality internalized and cancelled with VI. On the contrary, if firms bargain along the vertical chain the solution is a close replication of the VI result,

---

[2] See RUBINSTEIN A. (1982) or, for a good survey, PETROSJAN A. - ZENKEVICH A. (1996).

since firms symmetrically share the surplus, mimicking vertical collusion, as the NBS dictates. This makes for a result quite close to that of a vertical cartel even though the distribution of the joint surplus is a symmetric one.

Most of these conclusions are taken for granted in an environment in which there is market certainty, but do not apply in a stochastic environment. We shall see, in the following pages, that under uncertainty the results change according to which strategic variable is adopted by the D firm either with Stackelberg or with vertical bargaining (NBS). In the first case we shall find, for the D firm, a private superiority of quantity setting, which extends to the U firm if both stages of the production process show nonlinear costs. As we pointed out at the very beginning, price setting is quite common among firms selling to final consumers (D firms). For this reason, we shall be quite keen on the results obtained with this strategic policy.

We shall see that, with bargaining quantity and price setting, give rise to the same aggregate profits. However, price setting generates more equitable results along the vertical chain.

In other circumstances, *i.e.*, with convex costs price setting may turn out to be either superior or inferior to quantity setting according to the stochastic scenario and technology parameters.

The paper is organized as follows. In section 2 we go through Stackelberg vertical relationships. In section 3 we compare price and quantity settings. In section 4 NBS is investigated. In Section 5 we draw some concluding remarks.

2. - Outsourcing in a Stackelberg Framework

We consider a monopoly and a vertical production process. An intermediate input is needed to manufacture the final output sold to consumers. The technological relationship is one of perfect vertical complementarity, *i.e.*, one unit of the intermediate good is required for each unit of the final good.

We may feature two organizational arrangements: with VI only one firm owns both the output (D) and the input production

(U). With OS two distinct firms are respectively in the D and U sections and a market relationship is in between.

The vertical market relationship can be designed in at least two different modes: a non cooperative Stackelberg solution and a bargaining. We first examine the Stackelberg mode. In the next section we go through the bargaining solution.

In a vertical noncooperative relationship under certainty it is immaterial whether firm D is a price or a quantity setter. Things change with uncertainty. We know from literature (Leland, 1972; Klemperer and Meyer, 1986; Malliaris and Brock, 1982) that market uncertainty makes a difference as to the profit a monopolist gets according to whether the decision variable is price or quantity. Here, our aim is to see whether the choice of different controls has any effect in terms of the vertical arrangement (VI or OS) taken. As emphasized in the introduction, consumer goods producers publish price lists and stand ready to sell what the market requires. Price changes do not take place continuously[3] but only in a discrete way. In other words most firms set prices and adjust to the realization of uncertain market events.

Let us start modelling price setting. The demand function for the final good is uncertain and linear in the price (p), the size of the market (a) and the shock term (e):

(1) $$q = (a - p + e)$$

where q is the quantity sold. We assume that the additive shock term has zero expected value and constant, bounded second moment, *i.e.*,

(2) $$Ee = 0; \quad Ee^2 = \sigma^2$$

where E is the expectation operator.

---

[3] An example of continuously changing prices can be found in some services, like car rental or some goods like electricity. For instance, Avis quotes totally flexible prices, since it cannot adjust in the very short run the supply of cars. Electricity prices change over time yet in a discrete way.

In case of quantity setting the uncertain market demand is:

(3)
$$p = a - q + e$$

As far as the technology is concerned we adopt the same approach of Klemperer and Meyer (1986) for the D stage of production, while we keep linear technology for the U stage. Then total cost (C) in D is a quadratic function of quantity with c and d technological parameters:

(4)
$$C = c\,q + d\,q^2$$

In the U stage we assume that production has to bear a constant marginal cost z and that the intermediate input is sold to the D firm at price g.

2.1 Price Setting

In the case of price setting a simple proposition can be obtained:

PROPOSITION 1 The expected value of the profit of U is equal to the certainty profit, while for D it is lower for any finite level of the variance of the stochastic shock e. The higher is the degree of convexity of D costs the larger is the premium paid to uncertainty by D profits.

PROOF
Once we substitute p_S in the demand function we obtain the stochastic quantity that we plug in the profit of U:

(5)
$$\pi_U = g\,q - z\,q$$

Then, we take the expected value of π_U and first order conditions (FOCs) with respect to g and obtain:

(6)
$$\frac{\partial E\pi_U}{\partial g} = 0 \Rightarrow g = \frac{1}{2}(a - c + z)$$

As a result the optimal endogenous quantity is:

(7)
$$q^* = \frac{a + 4de - (c - 4e + z)}{4(1+d)}$$

Then, equilibrium expected profits of the two firms are[4]

(8)
$$E\pi^*_{DP} = \frac{A^2}{16(1+d)} - dEe^2 = \pi^*_{DP} - dEe^2$$

Then, for D, the expected profit is lower than the corresponding certainty profit (π^*_{DP}). For U we have:

(9)
$$E\pi^*_{UP} = \frac{A^2}{8(1+d)} = \pi^*_{UP}$$

which is equal to the corresponding certainty profit (π^*_{UP}). ∎

2.2 *Quantity Setting*

Here, again a simple result obtains:

PROPOSITION 2 From the comparison of price with quantity setting in the final stage (D) of the vertical chain, quantity setting turns out superior for the D firm. The U is indifferent since expected profit does not change. Moreover, D gains from a positive shock, while U does not.

PROOF
In this case the demand for the final good is:

(10)
$$p = a - q + e$$

Then, the profit of the D firm is:

(11)
$$\pi_D = p\, q - c\, q - d\, q^2 - g\, q$$

---

[4] We define $A = a - c - z$.

If we take the FOC of expected profit with respect to the quantity we get:

(12)
$$\frac{\partial E\pi_D}{\partial q} = 0 \Rightarrow q_S = \frac{a-c-g}{2(1+d)}$$

where the set quantity, equal to the its expected value, is a nonstochastic magnitude. The profit of the U firm is:

(13)
$$\pi_U = g\,q - z\,q$$

Following a similar procedure as in the previous subsection we obtain the price set by U:

(14)
$$\frac{\partial \pi U}{\partial g} = 0 \Rightarrow g_S = \frac{a-c+z}{2}$$

from which we have the quantity sold:

(15)
$$q^* = A/[4(1+d)]$$

The final good – stochastic – price is:

(16)
$$p = a + e - A/[4(1+d)]$$

The profit of U is nonstochastic since U takes from D the quantity set which is nonstochastic. Therefore:

(17)
$$\pi^*_{UQ} = A^2/[8(1+d)] = E\,\pi^*_{UQ}$$

while the realized profit of D is:

(18)
$$\pi^{R*}_{DQ} = \frac{A(A+4e)}{16(1+d)}$$

whose expected value is equal to

(19)
$$E\pi^*_{DQ} = \frac{A^2}{16(1+d)} = \pi^*_{DQ}$$

which is equal to the corresponding certainty level.

■

40

2.3 *Non Linear Costs in U*

In the case of nonlinear costs we may write the following:

COROLLARY 1 With non linear costs in both stages and price setting, also the expected profit of U is affected by the variance of the shock. Both U and D suffer in a way that depends on their respective cost parameters w and d.

PROOF
Further comparisons can be undertaken if we adopt non linear costs also in U, *i.e.*,

$$(20) \qquad CU = z\,q + w\,q^2$$

With price setting, expected profits of D are:

$$(21) \qquad E\pi_{DP} = \left[\frac{A^2 d}{4(2+2d+w)^2} - dEe^2\right]$$

while for U we have:

$$(22) \qquad E\pi_{UP} = \left[\frac{A^2}{4(2+2d+w)} - wEe^2\right]$$

If we calculate quantity setting expected profits we discover that they are equal to certainty profits, despite non linear costs. ∎

3. - Vertical Integration: Comparison between Quantity and Price Setting

Here we go through the case of VI for both price and quantity settings, using the same demand functions and the same U and D technologies. The profit of the VI monopoly is:

$$(23) \qquad \pi_{VI} = p\,q - c\,q - d\,q^2 - z\,q$$

since the intermediate good is internally transferred at its opportunity cost, equal to the marginal cost of production, *i.e.*, z. The result[5] can be summed up in:

PROPOSITION 3 With VI and market uncertainty expected profits are higher with quantity setting rather than with price setting.

PROOF
With price setting the FOC is:

$$\frac{\partial E\pi_{VIP}}{\partial p} = 0 \Rightarrow p_S = \frac{a+c+z+2ad}{2(1+d)}$$

Then, the optimal quantity is:

(24) $$q^* = A/[2\,(1+d)] + e$$

Expected profit is:

(25) $$E\pi_{VIP} = A^2/[4(1+d)] - Ee^2d$$

With quantity setting we get:

(26) $$\frac{\partial E\pi_{VIQ}}{\partial q} = 0 \Rightarrow q_S = \frac{A}{2(1+d)}$$

Substituting q_S in the demand function we get:

(27) $$p = a + e - A/[2(1+d)]$$

while equilibrium profit is:

(28) $$\pi_{VIQ} = [A(A+2e)]/[4(1+d)]$$

whose expected value is:

(29) $$E\pi_{VIQ} = A^2/[4(1+d)]$$

---

[5] This result closely replicates KLEMPERER P. - MAYER M. (1986).

equal to the certainty outcome. Comparison between the two settings leads to:

$$E\pi_{VIQ} - E\pi_{VIP} = Ee^2 d$$

As an extension, consider non linear costs also in U.
With price setting we have:

$$E\pi_{VIP} = (A^2)/[4(1 + d + w)] - (d + w)Ee^2 = \pi_{VIP} - (d + w)Ee^2$$

With quantity setting we get:

$$E\pi_{VIQ} = (A^2)/[4(1 + d + w)] = \pi_{VIQ}$$

When costs are non linear in U and D, the loss due to market uncertainty in terms of profits is the same no matter whether we have VI or OS.

4. - Vertical Bargaining

A common manner to feature vertical relationships is to figure out a bargaining between U and D firms. This arrangement may be easily modelled by the Nash Bargaining Solution and its refinements (Nash, 1950; Petrosjan and Zenkevich, 1996; Rubinstein, 1982, Kalai and Smorodinsky, 1975). With certainty the bargaining solution gives rise to aggregate profits equal to those of VI. Yet the distribution is symmetric among the two firms, while with VI there is no specific rule for the allocation of profits between the two vertical sections of production. In this sense a bargaining could provide a mechanism to fill the gap, in the absence of alternative ways. Nonetheless, the bargaining solution is quite common also for the modelling of vertical market relationships.

In this section we investigate a vertical relationship under uncertainty with price and quantity settings, assuming either symmetric or asymmetric baldness along the vertical chain. By baldness we mean the willingness to bear the risk of contract disruption, which may occur if the bargaining falls apart and outside options are chosen.

First we consider vertical bargaining solutions with symmetric baldness in U and D with price setting and quantity setting. Subsequently, we shall consider asymmetric baldness.

Demand structure is the same as above. As far as technologies are concerned we consider the simple case of linear settings. Finally, outside options are assumed equal to zero.

In this framework we are able to derive a novel result contained in the following:

PROPOSITION 4 With bargaining along the vertical chain, market uncertainty and symmetric baldness, quantity setting and price setting give rise to the same aggregate level of expected profits along the vertical chain. Under P setting the distribution of profits along the vertical chain is symmetric. With Q setting D makes larger profits than U. Then, U prefers P setting, while D prefers Q setting.

PROOF

Let's start with quantity setting. Demand replicates (3). D and U maximize expected profit. As a result the bargaining requires maximization of the geometric average of D and U expected profit[6]. This assumption is invariant between quantity and price setting. Here, we model uncertainty in a simple way, with only two states of nature whose probabilities are respectively α and $1 - \alpha$, while the associated shocks are e and $-e$. Therefore, we have:

$$E\pi_{DQ} = \alpha(a - c + e - g - q)q + (1 - \alpha)(a - c - e - g - q)q$$

---

[6] We may consider the maximization of the realized payoffs. The result would be quite different. The question about whether maximization of realized profits or expected profits are the right approaches cannot be entirely settled. No bargaining solution makes the payoffs of the two approaches coincide (See MAS-COLELL A. - WHINSTON M. - GREEN J., 1995, page 845). However, the bargaining on the realized payoffs is almost a replication of bargaining under certainty and, therefore, not very interesting. Then, we consider only the results of the bargaining on expected payoffs.

while

(30) $E\pi_{UQ} = q(g - z)$

The bargaining maximand is:

(31) $\Psi_Q = E\pi_{UQ} \; E\pi_{DQ}$

FOCs are:

$$(32) \qquad \left\{ \begin{array}{l} \dfrac{\partial \Psi_Q}{\partial q} = 0 \\[2mm] \dfrac{\partial \Psi_Q}{\partial g} = 0 \end{array} \right\}$$

From this we get equilibrium controls:

(33) $q^* = -1/2 \, (- a + c + e + z - 2\alpha e)$

and

(34) $g^* = 1/4(a - c + 5z - e + 2\alpha e)$

Therefore equilibrium expected profits are:

(35) $E\pi^*_{UQ} = 1/8(- a + c + e + z - 2e)^2$

(36) $E\pi^*_{DQ} = 1/8(a - c + 7e - z - 6\alpha e)(a - c - e - z + 2\alpha e)$

and it is easy to show that $E\pi^*_{DQ} > E\pi^*_{UQ}$.

Consider now price setting. We have that:

$E\pi^*_{UP} = \alpha(a + e - p)(g - z) + (1 - \alpha)(a - e - p)(g - z)$

and

$E\pi^*_{DP} = \alpha \, (a + e - p)(p - c - g) + (1 - \alpha)(a - e - p)(p - g - c)$

After the maximization of the corresponding maximand we get equilibrium profit, quantity and optimal controls p and g:

$$E\pi^*_{UP} = 1/8 \, (a - c + 3e - z - 2\alpha e)(a - c - e - z + 2\alpha e) = E\pi^*_{DP}$$

$$q^* = 1/2(a - c - z + 3e - 2\alpha e)$$

$$g^* = 1/4(a - c + 3z - e + 2\alpha e)$$

$$p^* = 1/2(a + c + z - e + 2\alpha e)$$

Some comparisons between price and quantity setting can be obtained. It can be easily seen that:

$$E\pi^*_{DP} + E\pi^*_{UP} = E\pi^*_{DQ} + E\pi^*_{UQ}$$

i.e., the sum of profits obtained in the two arrangements is the same. If we compare the profits accruing to the two sections (U and D) of production in the two settings we find that:

(37) $\quad E\pi^*_{UP} - E\pi^*_{UQ} = -0.5e \, (-1+\alpha) \, (a - c - e - z + 2\alpha e) \geq 0$

which means that U profits are larger with P setting, while

$$E\pi^*_{DP} - E\pi^*_{DQ} = 0.5e \, (-1+\alpha)(a - c - e - z + 2\alpha e) \leq 0$$

saying that D profits are larger with Q setting.
■

The above result departs from traditional conclusions we have obtained in the previous sections confirming the received wisdom that quantity setting is better for firms under uncertainty (Klemperer and Mayer, 1986). Our result is quite new and worth emphasizing.

First of all, aggregate expected profits are equal across the two marketing strategies, quantity and price setting. This result differs from the one obtained in the Stackelberg framework which confirms previous literature. However, the two sections of the vertical chain have different preferences as to the marketing policy that D should carry out *vis à vis* consumers. U wants P while D wants Q setting.

Then, we may wonder what happens if the two sections have different bargaining power, *i.e.* different baldness. The question is quite interesting since we know that in some sectors the U section is more powerful since there are less producers in U facing many producers in D. This may be the case of the few firms producing PC components, like Intel and Motorola which are quite powerful *vis à vis* PC producers which are in huge number. The opposite may happen in food production where the concentration in the D section is quite high while for most input components is much lower.

However, even if we extend the above bargaining[7] model and assume alternatively that U or D is balder, we always find the same ranking of preferences. There is always a preference by U for having P setting in the market for the final product, while D prefers quantity setting. This is consistent with the received wisdom in vertical integration theory that maintains that U prefers to face a highly competitive D market so as to be able to appropriate the entire surplus generated by the sale of the input to D firms.

Whenever the U section is able to condition the marketing behaviour of D price setting will be most likely, like in the PC industry. In other industries such as food we shall see a less competitive policy by the D section that will prefer a more comfortable Q setting. In some cases of specific inputs (Williamson, 1971; Grossman and Hart, 1986), the D party is more powerful, since the U party is captive or held-up. In other cases the reverse may apply with a U party which is more powerful. Notice that these results do not depend on the bargaining baldness of the two sections of production.

5. - Concluding Remarks

We have investigated VI and OS in a stochastic framework by

---

[7] Analytical results can be straightforwardly derived by the extension of the those presented for the symmetric case.

using two different equilibrium concepts: Stackelberg and Nash Bargaining Solution.

Stackelberg price setting, with market uncertainty and OS, is always inferior for the D firm. If we allow for non linear costs in U, inferiority extends to the U firm, that prefers the D firm to set the quantity rather than the price.

An analogous result can be found with VI. With bargaining, aggregate expected profits are equal regardless of whether price or quantity setting is adopted. However, with price setting the distribution of expected profits along the vertical chain is not symmetric: U is better off while D is worse off.

This makes for a departure from received results on price and quantity setting under uncertainty, which maintained that quantity, is always superior to price setting for firms. When vertically disintegrated production processes are considered, price setting may be preferred by one section of the vertical chain.

BIBLIOGRAPHY

ACEMOGLU D. - AGHION P. - GRIFFITH R. - ZILIBOTTI F., «Vertical Integration and Technology: Theory and Evidence», *CEPR, Discussion Paper*, no. 5258, 2005.

ACEMOGLU D. - JOHNSON S. - MITTON T., «Determinants of Vertical Integration: Finance, Contracts and Regulation», *NBER, Working Paper*, no. 11424, 2005.

AMITI M. - WEI S.J., «Fear of Service Outsourcing: is it Justified?», *IMF, Working Paper*, no. 04/186, 2004.

ANTRAS P. - HELPMAN E., «Global Sourcing», *CEPR, Discussion Paper*, no. 4170, 2004.

ARMOUR H.O. - TEECE D.J., «Vertical Integration and Technological Innovation», *Review of Economics and Statistics*, no. 62, 1980, pages 490-494.

BHAGWATI J. - PANAGARIYA A. - SRINIVASAN T.N., «The Muddles over Outsourcing», *Journal of Economic Perspectives*, no. 18, 2004, pages 93-114.

BANERJEE S. - LIN P., «Vertical Research Joint Ventures», *International Journal of Industrial Organization*, no. 19, 2001, pages 285-302.

BROCAS I., «Vertical Integration and the Incentive to Innovate», *International Journal of Industrial Organization*, no. 21, 2003, pages 457-605.

BUEHLER S. - SCHMUTZLER A., «Who Integrates?», *CEPR, Discussion Paper*, no. 4066, 2003.

GROSSMAN G.M. - HELPMAN E., «Integration versus Outsourcing in Industry Equilibrium», *Quarterly Journal of Economics*, no. 117, 2002, pages 85-120.

GROSSMAN S.J. - HART O.D., «The Costs and Benefits of Ownership: A Theory of Vertical and Lateral Integration», *Journal of Political Economy*, no. 94, 1986, pages 691-719.

KALAI E. - SMORODINSKY M., «Other Solutions to Nash's Bargaining Problem», *Econometrica*, no. 43, 1975, pages 513-518.

KLEMPERER P. - MEYER M., «Price Competition versus Quantity Competition: The Role of Uncertainty», *RAND, Journal of Economics*, no. 17, 1986, pages 618-638.

LAMBERTINI L. - ROSSINI G., «Vertical Integration and Differentiation in an Oligopoly with Process Innovating R&D», Department of Economics University of Bologna, *Working Paper*, no. 468, 2003.

— — - — —, «Endogenous Outsourcing and Vertical Integration with Process R&D», forthcoming in *Economics of Innovation and New Technology*, 2008.

LELAND H., «Theory of the Firm Facing Uncertain Demand», *American Economic Review*, no. 62, 1972, no. 278-291.

MALLIARIS A.G. - BROCK W.A., *Stochastic Methods in Economics and Finance*, North Holland, Amsterdam, 1982.

MAS-COLELL A. - WHINSTON M. - GREEN J., *Microeconomic Theory*, Oxford University Press, Oxford, 1995.

McLAREN J., «Supplier Relations and the Market Context: A Theory of Handshakes», *Journal of International Economics*, no. 48, 1999, pages 121-138.

— —, «Globalization and Vertical Structure», *American Economic Review*, no. 90, 2000, pages 239-1254.

NASH J., «The Bargaining Problem», *Econometrica*, no. 28, 1950, pages 155-162.

NEMOTO J. - GOTO M., «Technological Externalities and Economies of Vertical Integration in the Electric Utility Market», *International Journal of Industrial Organization*, no. 22, 2004, pages 67-82.

PEPALL L. - NORMAN G., «Product Differentiation and Upstream-Downstream Relations», *Journal of Economics and Management Strategy*, no. 10, 2001, pages 201-233.

PERRY M.K., «Vertical Integration: Determinants and Effects», in SCHMALENSEE R. - WILLING R. (eds.), *Handbook of Industrial Organization*, vol. 1, Amsterdam, North-Holland, 1989, pages 103-255.

PETROSJAN L.A. - ZENKEVICH N.A., *Game Theory*, World Scientific, New York, 1996.

ROSSINI G., «Outsourcing with Labor Management». *Economic Systems*, no. 29, pages 455-466, 2005.

— —, «Pitfalls in Private and Social Incentives of Vertical Cross-border Integration and Disintegration», *Review of International Economics*, no. 15, 2007, pages 932-947.

ROSSINI G. - RICCIARDI D., «Vertical Disintegration in a Sample of Italian Firms: Some Empirical Evidence», *Review of Economic Conditions in Italy*, no. 3, 2005, pages 517-532.

RUBINSTEIN A., «Perfect Equilibrium in a Bargaining Model», *Econometrica*, no. 50, 1982, pages 97-109.

SLADE M.E., «Beer and the Tie: Did Divestiture of Brewer Owned Public Houses Lead to Higher Beer Prices?», *The Economic Journal*, no. 108, 1998a, pages 565-602.

— —, «Strategic Motives for Vertical Separation: Evidence from Retail Gasoline Markets», *Journal of Law Economics and Organization*, no. 14, 1998b, pages 84-113.

SPENGLER J., «Vertical Integration and Antitrust Policy», *Journal of Political Economy*, no. 58, 1950, pages 347-352.

TEECE D.J., *Vertical Integration and Vertical Divestiture in the US Oil Industry*, Institute for Energy Studies, Stanford (CA), 1976.

TIROLE J., *The Theory of Industrial Organization*, MIT Press, Cambridge (MA), 1988.

WILLIAMSON O.E., «The Vertical Integration of Production: Market Failure Considerations», *American Economic Review*, no. 61, 1971, pages 112-123.

Contagious "Social Market Enterprises": The Role of Fair Traders

Leonardo Becchetti - Giuseppina Gianfreda*

'Tor Vergata' University, Rome   University of Tuscia, Viterbo

One of the effects of the introduction of fair trade goods is that of triggering socially responsible imitation of profit maximising sellers and distributors, thereby creating a consumer driven market mechanism which promotes equity and inclusion. To proof our claim we analyze the effects of a fair trader's entry in a differentiation model where the profit maximizing incumbent may react in prices and social responsibility and its position on the segment of social responsibility needs to be advertised at some cost. We outline complementarity and substitution effects among relevant variables and explore incumbent's incentives to cheat on his ethical stance. [JEL Classification: L11, L31]

1. - Introduction

In the traditional welfare economics approach problems of negative externalities generated by productive units, inequality of opportunities and underprovision of public goods where tackled by the action of "enlightened" domestic institutions. This framework adequately represents the reality of the pre-globalisation economic system. In such system checks and

* *<Becchetti@economia.uniroma2.it>*, Faculty of Economics; *<ggianfreda@unitus.it>*, Faculty of Political Science. The Authors thank F. Adriani, S. Anderson, M. Bagella, K. Basu, R. Cellini, L. Debenedictis, M. Fenoaltea, B. Frey, P. Garella, I. Hasan, L. Lambertini, S. Martin, N. Phelps, G. Piga and P. Scaramozzino, M.E. Tessitore, P. Wachtel, C. Whilborg and all participants to the 1st ECINEQ Conference held in Palma de Majorca and to seminars held at the XV Villa Mondragone Conference, at SOAS in London, at the Copenhagen Business School and the Universities of Catania, Bologna, Macerata, Milano Bicocca, Trento and Verona for the useful comments and suggestions received. The usual disclaimer applies.

balances among corporations, domestic institutions and trade unions ensured the joint pursuit of economic development and social cohesion, thereby avoiding socially disruptive levels of inequality. The global integration of labour and product markets has significantly weakened the bargaining power of domestic institutions and trade unions. Corporations can now operate globally, with the risk of generating a "race to the bottom" among domestic fiscal authorities and workers' representatives in order to attract job opportunities and direct investment.

In this perspective the rise of bottom-up pressure of "concerned" consumers and investors may therefore be viewed as a sort of endogenous reaction of the socioeconomic system facing the excess bargaining power of global corporations: consumers and investors vote with their portfolio by looking not just at price and quality, but also at the social value incorporated in the products.

In this respect, one of the most interesting and novel features of contemporary product markets is the competitive race between traditional profit maximizing producers and a new generation of socially responsible (hereafter also SR) entrants whose main goal is not profit maximization but the introduction of elements of social and environmental sustainability in their products or processes.

A typical example of the latter is represented by fair trade importers (from now on simply fair traders). Fair traders (hereafter also FTs) introduce in the market food and textile goods produced accordingly to a set of socially and environmentally responsible criteria.[1] FT producers in LDCs have started from

---

[1] These criteria, defined by the Fair Trade Federation (FTF), are: *i)* paying a fair wage in the local context; *ii)* offering employees opportunities for advancement (including investment in local public goods); *iii)* providing equal employment opportunities for all people, particularly the most disadvantaged; *iv)* engaging in environmentally sustainable practices; *v)* being open to public accountability; *vi)* building long-term trade relationships; *vii)* providing healthy and safe working conditions within the local context; *viii)* providing technical and financial assistance (price stabilisation insurance services and anticipated financing arrangements which reduce financial constraints) to producers whenever possible. Further information on Fair Trade may be found, among others, on the following websites: *www.eftafairtrade.org* (European Fair Trade Association) and *www.fairtradefederation.com* (Fair Trade Federation).

niche market shares which have progressively increased in the last years, also due to contagion effects on traditional profit maximizing competitors.[2] From this point of view one of the most surprising events its the decision by Nestlè on October 2005 to produce its first FT product. In the press release the company's choice is explained by the fact that the sector of SR consumption is promising and is expected to have a two-digit growth in the next years. Another surprising fact which justifies the importance of looking at competition in this new industry is that the highest share of FT coffee sales in 2006 is from a well known profit maximizing imitator (Starbucks).

Given the above mentioned features we define fair traders as "social market enterprises". They are social in the sense that their main goal is not profit maximisation but the promotion of market inclusion of marginalized producers. They are *social market enterprises* and not just *social enterprises* as they do not operate in protected sectors nor have they been delegated the provision of social services by the Government in areas in which there are natural monopolies. On the contrary they operate in sectors in which they compete with standard profit maximizing companies.

Adriani and Becchetti (2004) and Becchetti and Costantino (2007) have shown that FT criteria contain eight bottom-up mechanisms with which the civil society may amend relevant market failures. More specifically, the premium paid on commodity prices provides price stabilization mechanisms and helps to restore competitive prices from the monopsonistic framework in which small primary product producers usually exchange with

---

[2] In 2003 the European Fairtrade Labeling Organization, FLO, certified 315 organizations, representing almost 500 first level producer structures and around 900,000 families of farmers and workers from 40 countries (MOORE G., 2004). FT products were sold by 2,700 dedicated outlets (called world shops) and by 43,000 supermarkets across Europe (7,000 in the US). The 2005 EFTA (European Fair Trade Association) report documents that total FT sales experienced a yearly growth rate of 20 percent per year from 200 to 2005. Some FT products have achieved significant market shares in specific segments such as the ground coffee market in the EU (2%), the banana market in Switzerland (49%), the roast and ground coffee market in the UK (20%) and the tea market in Germany (2.5%) (MOORE G., 2004; CAFEDIRECT, 2003).

monopolistic or oligopsonistic trade intermediaries.[3] The price premium, together with the prefinancing mechanism aimed at reducing credit rationing of small uncollateralised producers and dependence from local monopolistic moneylenders, may be viewed as forms of international antitrust action with which the civil society partially fills the gap represented by the lack of cross country antitrust rules. Destination of part of the price premium to investment in factors fostering local development and establishment of long run partnerships, which provide export and business angel services to local producers, contribute to make fair trade an interesting and powerful instrument of growth and inclusion.

One of the most relevant and partially unexplored potential effects of fair traders' entry in product markets is the indirect positive effect on the diffusion of socially responsible imitation among its profit maximizing competitors. We do not enter in the evaluation of pros and cons of FT development policies. Our specific goal is to start from their existence and evaluate conditions under which, in a duopoly, fair trader's entry triggers partial socially responsible imitation in the profit maximizing incumbent.

Another crucial issue in FT is asymmetric information. SR cannot be easily verified by consumers who need to rely on what producers say about it. For fair traders SR is one of the main competitive factors and therefore they should have strong incentives to maintain their reputation on this issue. On the other hand maximizing competitors might be tempted to cheat on the issue by declaring to move toward SR without paying the cost of it.

---

[3] Support for the existence of monopsonistic labour markets for unskilled workers, not just in developing but also in developed countries, is provided by several authors (MANNING A., 2003; CARD D. - KRUEGER A.B., 2000). MANNING A. (2003) argues that it is not necessary to think of the mining or mill town in the early days of the Industrial Revolution to conceive the existence of monopsony or of thin labour markets. Labour markets may be thin not just in presence of a single employer, but also when employers are few and collude or in presence of geographical distance and labour differentiation. The first two cases may well apply to producers in developing countries. Evidence of employers' excess market power in developing countries is provided by several empirical papers (EL HAMIDI F. - TERRELL K., 2001; CAMARGO J., 1984; GONZAGA G. et AL., 1999; CARNEIRO F., 2002; LEMOS S., 2004).

Our work deals with these issues and is divided into five sections (including introduction and conclusions). In the second section we outline our product differentiation model describing characteristics of the two producers and the market segment. In the third section we analyse the profit maximizing producer (hereafter PMP) reaction to the entry of a socially responsible producer (such as the fair trader) in a market space, in which differentiation depends on the ethical stance of production, information is asymmetric and the PMP position on the ethical segment needs to be advertised at some costs. In the third section we evaluate the incentive of the PMP to cheat on SR imitation under different model assumptions.

2. - The Model

2.1 *The Basic Assumptions*

Most of the hypotheses in the model which follows are derived from Becchetti, Giallonardo and Tessitore (2007) and Becchetti and Solferino (2008). We add to them the hypothesis of informational asymmetry on the SR quality of the product and the possibility for the producer to advertise it at some cost. We outline model features by defining producers, market space and consumers.

The Production Side

The monopolist profit maximizer

The monopolist transforms raw materials received from unskilled producers in the South[4] paid with a monopsony wage

---

[4] Almost 100 percent of the first level producer associations selling raw material and intermediate products in the fair trade chain are from Latin America, Africa and Asia. We therefore generically identify them as producer from the South in the model.

(w).[5] He maximizes profits by fixing a price P_A for his product which is sold to consumers in the North.

The fair trader

We assume in this benchmark model that "there are no free lunches in ethical responsibility" and we abstract from asymmetric information on the quality of the FT product. The Fair trader's criteria of action are those described in the introduction. We "stylise" these features by assuming that the entrant sells his product at zero profit[6] and transfers a fixed margin $\bar{s}$[7] (after paying the monopsony wage w) which is needed to comply with all the Fair Trade criteria described at footnote 1 and commented in the introduction (provision of local public goods, premium on the monopsony wage, creation of a long term partnership through the provision of export services, etc.).[8] The zero profit condition of the entrant is therefore: $P_B = w (1 + \bar{s})$.

---

[5] The reason for not considering in this paper the impact of fair trade on South labour markets is explained at footnote 8.

[6] Fair trade associations usually have zero or negligible profits. This condition is often statutory since most of them take the form of cooperatives. For simplicity we assume here that they are zero profit. The assumption of small positive profits would not change the substance of our model based on the assumption that profit maximisation is not the goal of FT producers.

[7] We take the fair trader as an example of socially responsible producer and identify social responsibility in the resources transferred to producers in the South. Our model may be generalised and applied also to "environmentally concerned" producers by assuming that the adoption of environmentally responsible production processes increases costs exactly as in our fair trader's example.

[8] Fair Trade criteria of action imply a series of initiatives in support of producers in the South (prefinancing, provision of local public goods, a premium as a minimum wage measure against monopsonistic labour markets, export services, price stabilisation mechanisms, training and counselling etc.). On the premise that these initiatives are not costless, we stylise all of them in the model into an additional cost component (the transfer s) that the FT sends to the producer in the South. Hence, the transfer s is not related to the minimum wage only and the reason for its existence does not disappear, even in case of end of the monopsony on the labour markets.

Second, the FT's dimension with respect to world Markets and the multiple directions of his action, are such that the decision of a single FT to send s does not reduce its need in the future for further producers. A very effective and concentrated action in one area may reduce the monopsony problem, but it does not eliminate the other reasons of the transfer. Hence, it is not unreasonable to

The Market Space

The entry of the FT into the market has the effect of creating a new market space along an "ethical" unit segment (Graph 1). Location on the left extreme corresponds to the choice of no transfer to South producers in addition to the monopsony wage ($s = 0$), while location on the right extreme corresponds to the choice of an exogenous transfer under the assumption of full

GRAPH 1

THE ETHICAL PRODUCT DIFFERENTIATION
AND THE ASYMMETRIC COSTS OF ETHICAL DISTANCE

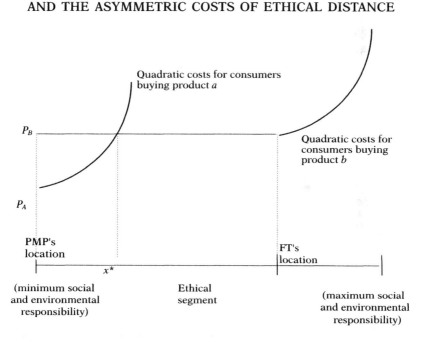

Legend: moving to the left of the ethical segment implies choosing a product below one's own ethical standards (and therefore is costly) while moving to right implies choosing a product above one's own ethical standards (and therefore does not give any added psychological benefit or cost to the buyer).

consider that the individual FT decision to send s does not eliminate the aggregate problem of the inclusion of small uncollateralized producers with low bargaining power in the South. These considerations led us to focus on the interaction between FT and incumbent without modelling the effects of the s transfer in the South.

compliance with the Fair Trade criteria mentioned in the introduction $(s = \bar{s})$. Within these two extreme choices both producers dispose of a set of (a) strategies in social responsibility where $a \in [0, 1]$. Hence their final choice may be generalised as their $(a \; \bar{s})$ position on the segment. This allows them to locate in any point of the segment if they want.

Informational asymmetry on the ethical content of the product

Consumers have no knowledge on the existence/characteristics of the products other than the information provided by producers. By paying advertising costs competitors may signal to consumers the producer's positioning on the ethical segment. We focus only on advertising costs related to the ethical content of the products. Costs associated to the information about the existence and the other features of products are just treated as part of the total costs of production.

We also introduce an asymmetry between the FT and the PMP, reflecting a current practice in ethical product markets, *i.e.* the fact that FTs do not engage in traditional advertising activities and rely on other forms of communication[9].

In terms of our model, the lack of advertising by the FT is explained by the fact that, once the FT existence is known, its SR stance does not need to be communicated to the market. The FT activity is expected to be "ethical" since a departure from the ethical stance would lead to a loss of reputation making the FT survivorship possible only by behaving like the PMP, which is at odds with its motivation for entering the market. The same is not true for the PMP, whose production does not need to have SR features by definition. On the contrary, the PMP is traditionally not engaged in ethical production. He does move on the ethical

---

[9] Descriptive and empirical analyses on the FT market show that FT producers do not spend at all in advertising, while investing in education and promotion of consumers awareness of FT products. This behaviour is rational since BECCHETTI L. - ROSATI F. (2007) show that the demand for FT products is strongly affected by awareness of FT criteria which, in turn, is increased by purchasing habits in FT specialised outlets (worldshops).

segment in order to conquer market shares, and he needs to advertise the novelty of the SR characteristics of his product.

More specifically, in the model, given a position "*a*" on the SR segment, and given the intensity of advertising $\beta \in [0,1]$ on the ethical content of the product whose marginal cost is $c \in [0,1]$, we assume that the SR of the PMP perceived by the market is equal to $a\beta$.

Model parametrisation

In order to provide reasonable parametric assumptions to our model (and, in particular, to allow the relationship between *w* and β to make sense) we take as a benchmark the actual behaviour of FTs on the markets. FT international criteria fix, in the market of agricultural commodities such as coffee and cocoa, a standard contingent premium on market prices adopted by all local organisations. In cocoa and coffee markets for the last 20 years the premium reached a maximum of around 100 percent in market downturns, and a minimum of 5 percent in market upturns (see Graphs 2 and 3). We therefore, and without lack of generality, normalise *w* = 1 (but continue to indicate it as *w* for expositional

GRAPH 2

MONTHLY MARKET PRICE OF COCOA BEANS
(US dollars per 1000 Kgs)

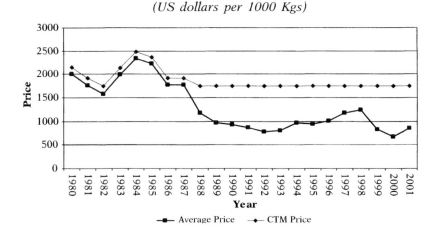

GRAPH 3

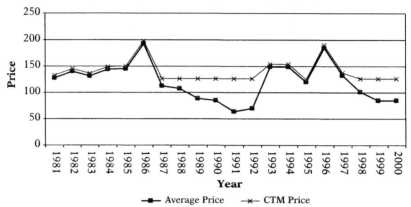

MONTHLY MARKET PRICE OF COFFEE
(cents of US dollars per 1000 pounds)

Legend: CTM price: fair trade price charged by the leading Italian fair trade importer according to international FT standards.

clarity and convenience). In this way both costs of SR advertising and transfers to the South are a share of total costs for the PMP. Based on what shown in Graphs 2 and 3, by setting fair trader's location to $\bar{s} = 1$ we fall in the case of market price downturn, while, if we set $\bar{s} = .05$, we are in case of market price downturns and minimum FT premium.

The Demand Side

Consumers

   Consumers are assumed to have inelastic, unit demands, heterogeneous preferences on social responsibility and to be uniformly distributed along the unit line (a standard feature in product differentiation models).[10]

---

   [10] Import duties, value added taxes and transportation costs are obviously part of total costs of importers of agricultural products from the South. In this paper, though, they do not add any insight to our main findings and are therefore omitted from the model.

60

The specificity of this product differentiation model is that a different position in the interval for consumers does not imply differences in physical distance or in product characteristics, but in the psychological perception of the ethical value of the good. The consideration of ethical instead of physical distance makes a difference in at least two ways. First, consistently with our concept of ethical distance, the cost of moving along the line segment is positive only for those going from a more ethical to a less ethical point. As a consequence, by considering the extreme right of the segment as the most ethical position, consumers move without costs to the right, while they incur in costs proportional to the "ethical" distance anytime they move to the left.[11] This explains why costs are increasing in the distance between consumers and PMP location for consumers buying from the PMP in Graph 1.

We assume that consumers utilities are decreasing in product price and also in the distance between consumer's ethical stance and the ethical value incorporated in the purchased product. The psychological cost of buying a product which is below one's own ethical standards is t times the ethical distance so that consumer's welfare is

$$W = Rp - Pi - t (x - a\beta)^2 \text{ for } (x - a\beta) \geq 0 \text{ or}$$

$$W = Rp - Pi \text{ for } (x - a\beta) \leq 0$$

where Rp is the common consumers' "conditional" reservation price, that is, the maximum price they are willing to pay in case of zero costs of ethical distance and x denotes generic consumer location, Pi is the price of the product sold by the ith seller, "a" is the product ethical content, β is the amount of advertising on the ethical content of the product which is incorporated in it, x is a generic consumers' location, while t is a multiplicative coefficient mapping the cost of ethical distance into consumer disutility.

---

[11] The rationale for these assumptions is that moving to the left implies choosing a product below one's own ethical standards (which is psychologically costly), while moving to the right implies choosing a product above one's own ethical standards (which therefore we assume it does not give any psychological cost to the buyer).

After the specification of the FT's behaviour and of the consumer's position on the segment, the cost of ethical distance has a clear monetary counterpart. When the producer is located at the right of the consumer this cost represents the distance in monetary terms between the transfer which is considered fair by the consumer (indicated by his location on the segment) and the transfer provided by the producer (indicated by the producer's location on the segment).

The ethical features of the model

Given the model characteristics, it is clear that the SR feature coincides with the application of the set of specific FT criteria along the value chain. These criteria promote a series of actions to foster inclusion of South producers with low bargaining power in international markets. Hence, SR is related to what happens in the productive process and in the overall value chain behind the product, more than to the intrinsic features of the product sold.

3.1 *Simultaneous Price SR Choice of the PMP after FT Entry on the Market*

In this version of the model the profit maximising producer is a monopolistic incumbent set at the extreme of the ethical segment (he chooses the strategy $a = 0$). An "orthodox" Fair Trader enters and places himself at $\bar{s}$. The PMP ethical location is not fixed and he can react both in prices and ethical location. Consumers are imperfectly informed and the incumbent's SR choice needs to be advertised at some cost.

The zero profit FT assumption implies that $P_B = w + w\bar{s}$, where P_B is the price of the FT product and w can be interpreted as a parameter including all production costs. The consumers' indifference condition is then given by the following equality: $P_A + t (x - a\beta)^2 = P_B$, where $P_B \geq P_A$ ensures nonzero market share to the PMP. From that expression the PMP market share after the FT's entry can be easily derived as

$$x^* = \sqrt{\frac{P_B - P_A}{t}} + a\beta$$

After such entry, the PMP can change his position on the ethical segment, *i.e.* he can choose $a \neq 0$. In order to signal the ethical content of his production, the PMP incurs in an extra-cost "*c*", which is the unit cost of the extra-advertising, *i.e.* the multiplicative unit cost component for a given SR advertising strength β. At this stage, β is treated as exogenous.[12] After the FT's entry, the incumbent will then choose price and ethical location in order to maximize:

(1)[13]
$$\max_{P_A, a} \pi = \left[P_A - w(1 + a\overline{s}) - c\beta \right] \left(\sqrt{\frac{P_B - P_A}{t}} + a\beta \right)$$

s.t.
$a, \in [0, 1]$, $P_A \in [w, P_B]$ and $\beta = 0$ if $a^* = 0$.

The two first-order conditions are[14]:

(2)
$$2\left(\frac{P_B - P_A}{t} \right) - \frac{P_A}{t} + \frac{w}{t} + \frac{w a\overline{s}}{t} + \frac{c\beta}{t} + 2a\beta\sqrt{\frac{P_B - P_A}{t}} = 0$$

(3)
$$P_A - w - \frac{w\overline{s}}{\beta}\sqrt{\frac{P_B - P_A}{t}} - 2w a\overline{s} - c\beta = 0$$

Combining *(2)* and *(3)*, imposing the $(P_B - P_A) \geq 0$ constraint and solving for P_A yields the following optimal price for *a*:

---

[12] The assumption will be removed in section 3.3.
[13] Consider that the profit maximising producer market share at his right goes to zero if the price is higher ($P_A > P_B$) or is undetermined if ($P_A = P_B$). In this second case we assume that the certainty of conquering all consumers at his right is preferred to the indeterminacy situation.
[14] Second order conditions for a maximum are always met if $a \geq 0$ or if

$$c < \frac{w\overline{s}}{\beta} + \left(1 + \frac{1}{4} \frac{w\overline{s}}{\beta^2 t} \right)$$

(4)
$$P_A^* = P_B - \frac{(w\bar{s})^2}{4t\beta^2}$$

Plugging *(4)* into *(3)* gives the optimal ethical stance of the PMP producer:

(5)
$$a^* = \frac{1}{2} - \frac{3}{8}\frac{w\bar{s}}{t\beta^2} - \frac{c\beta}{2w\bar{s}}$$

for $a^* \in [0,1]$.

From *(4)* we observe that, *as far as the solution for ethical imitation is an interior optimum*, optimal prices are increasing in both t and β as the two variables (consumers' cost of ethical distance and effectiveness of SR advertising) raise gains from ethical imitation, thereby allowing the PMP to charge a higher price. Moreover, from the inspection of *(4)*, we also identify a *dual effect of FT transfer on PMP price*.

The negative effect arises because a higher maximum transfer implies a higher impact of PMP's SR imitation on costs, thereby reducing optimal ethical imitation and prices. The positive effect depends on the complementarity between ethical stance, on the one side, and FT and PMP prices, on the other side. Finally, the price non-negativity condition is met if

$$\beta \geq \frac{w\bar{s}}{2\sqrt{tw(1+\bar{s})}}$$

The inspection of *(5)* shows the presence of a dual effect of advertising effectiveness on SR imitation and a dual effect of FT transfer on SR imitation in presence of advertising costs.

Dual effect of advertising effectiveness on SR imitation

a^* varies both positively and negatively with β, due to the concurrence of both a complementarity and a substitution effect. On the one hand, β increases the marginal effect of ethical production. On the other hand, it competes with "a" on the side of costs, by absorbing resources that otherwise could be used to increase the level of socially responsible imitation a.

Dual effect of FT transfer on SR imitation with SR advertising costs

It is also worth noting that "*a*" varies both inversely and positively with $w\bar{s}$. On the one hand, a higher transfer implies a higher impact of ethical imitation on costs, and this explains its negative effect on the PMP's SR imitation. On the other hand, an increase in the transfer lowers the relative cost of SR advertising ($c/w\bar{s}$), generating enough margin, in terms of potential PMP price increase, necessary to absorb extra advertising costs. By the same token, as c increases, the substitution effect is strengthened even though the relative cost of "*a*" ($\bar{s}/c$) declines and, *ceteris paribus*, this tends to reduce optimal ethical imitation.

3.2 *A Parametric Analysis of Market Equilibrium under World Commodity Price Downturns and Upturns*

The possibility of identifying quantitative intervals for many of the model parameters from the existing empirical evidence helps us formulating a parametric analysis which can provide useful insights as to the impact of the advertising effort and marginal cost of advertising on ethical imitation.

Our goal is to illustrate the region of parameters for which the interior optimum solutions apply. To begin with we normalize w to 1 without loss of generality. Reasonable values for $\bar{s}$ come from the FT experience of the last two decades where the transfer ranged from around a 100 percent increase over the coffee and cocoa commodity market prices under commodity market downturns to a 5 percent markup under booming commodity market prices (Graphs 2 and 3).

We therefore examine two different scenarios considering respectively the following values of $\bar{s}$ for the case of extreme market downturn ($\bar{s} = 1$) and market upturn ($\bar{s} = .05$).

Graphs 4 and 6 plot the optimal values of ethical imitation as a function of advertising efforts for market downturn under the assumption that marginal costs of extra advertising are alternatively $c = .05$ and $c = .01$. Since $w = 1$ the costs are conveniently parametrised in terms of total non advertising costs. In market downturn ethical imitation is always increasing in β and is nonzero only for high values of β (Graphs 4 and 6). In particular, for $c = .05$, a^* turns positive when $β = .89$ and, for $c = .01$, when $β = .87$ approximately — while, for $c = .1$, a^* turns positive when $β = .91$. Hence, in market downturn, the complementarity effect between a and $β$ prevails on the substitution effect.

The same is not true for market upturns (Graphs 5 and 7)[15], in which a is at first increasing in β and then decreasing, the turning points occurring at $β = .3$, for $c = .05$, and at $β = .2$, for $c = .01$ The interpretation is that, when the transfer is very low, *the relative cost of advertising SR imitation is relatively higher so that the substitution effect prevails.* In terms of *(5)*, if the transfer is

GRAPHS 4-7

SR IMITATION AND SR ADVERTISING EFFECTIVENESS UNDER COMMODITY MARKET PRICE MINIMA (4 AND 6) AND MAXIMA (5 AND 7)

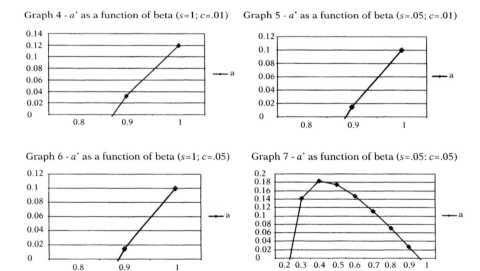

Graph 4 - a^* as a function of beta ($s=1$; $c=.01$)   Graph 5 - a^* as a function of beta ($s=.05$; $c=.01$)

Graph 6 - a^* as a function of beta ($s=1$; $c=.05$)   Graph 7 - a^* as function of beta ($s=.05$: $c=.05$)

---

[15] As far as $c = 0.1$, second order conditions are not met.

GRAPHS 8-9

SR IMITATION AND SR ADVERTISING COSTS
WITH FULL ADVERTISING EFFECTIVENESS
UNDER COMMODITY MARKET PRICE MINIMA (8) AND MAXIMA (9)

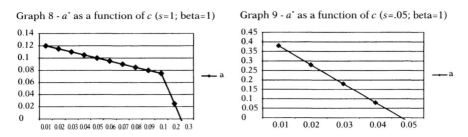

Graph 8 - a^* as a function of c ($s=1$; beta=1)   Graph 9 - a^* as a function of c ($s=.05$; beta=1)

very low, the third member on the right hand side gets very high. Furthermore, the optimal a^* is positive from .198 for $c = .01$ and, from $\beta = .02$ to $\beta = .95$, for $c = .05$.

Graphs 8-9 plot optimal ethical imitation as a function of the marginal costs of extra advertising for market downturn and upturn respectively with c ranging from .01 to .4 under the assumption that β is equal to unity. In both cases, the decreasing line gets steeper after .1. In market downturn, a^* stays positive for $c < .25$, while, in market upturn, a^* stays positive only as long as $c < .048$.

3.3 *Simultaneous Choice on Price, Ethical Location and Advertising by the PMP*

In this version of the model the profit maximising producer is a monopolistic incumbent set at the extreme of the ethical segment (he chooses the strategy $a = 0$). An "orthodox" Fair Trader enters and places himself at $\bar{s}$. The main difference with respect to what analysed above is that the PMP can react not only in prices, but also in ethical location and advertising effort of his SR choice.

PROPOSITION 1: when the profit maximizing producer reacts in prices, ethical location and advertising effort of his SR choice to the FT entry we observe that: *i)* SR imitation and full advertising effort are strict complements in the optimal PMP behaviour; *ii)* there is complementarity between PMP optimal price and ethical location; *iii)* for given values of the extra cost of SR advertising, compatible with non zero PMP's SR imitation, the latter is inverse U-shaped with respect to the FT transfer.

We now remove the hypothesis of exogenous β and allow the PMP to decide the amount of extra-advertising he wants to invest in communicating his ethical production to consumers. The PMP maximization problem is now:

(6) $$\max_{P_A,a,\beta} \pi = \left[P_A - w(1+a\bar{s}) - c\beta\right]\left(\sqrt{\frac{P_B - P_A}{t}} + a\beta\right)$$

s.t.: $a, \beta \in [0, 1]$, $P_A \in [w, P_B]$

Maximizing *(6)* on β adds the following to the first order conditions:

(7) $$P_A - w - wa\bar{s} - \frac{c}{a}\sqrt{\frac{P_B - P_A}{t}} - 2c\beta = 0$$

Combining *(7)*, *(2)* and *(3)* gives the optimum relation between *a* and β:

(8) $$a^* = \frac{c\beta^*}{w\bar{s}}$$

equation *(8)* highlights the complementarity between *a* and β: the more the producer invests in communicating the ethical stance of his product, the higher is *a*. Furthermore, the higher the transfer, the lower the ethical content of the PMP product. In both cases, it is noteworthy that once that optimal advertising effort is taken into account (*i.e.* resources to be devoted to advertising are decided upon) the substitution effect between *a* and β no longer exists.

As a and β do not depend on a straightforward combination of the parameters, algebraic solutions for those variables do not allow an immediate evaluation of optimal values. On the other hand, we are constrained by a limited range of possible values for the parameters, so that the optimization problem makes sense only for that range of values. We than opted for calibration[16]. In particular, we look at maxima of the profit function within the following ranges for relevant parameters: $\bar{s}$ [1, .05] (consistently with empirical evidence on FT transfer, documented by Graphs 2 and 3), c [.05, .01], w normalized to 1 and "ethical neutrality" (t = 1).[17] For $c >$ .05, extra costs of SR advertising are too high and the solution $a = 0$ always dominates internal solutions. Indeed, if the PMP can choose its advertising effort, the range of values for the exogenous parameters for which ethical imitation is profit maximizing does shrink.

For each combination of s and c in the chosen range of values we calculate profits according to *(1)*, using all possible combinations of values for the endogenous variables.

In doing so we report our results for the following admissible parametric intervals of the relevant variables: $a \in$ [0, .5],[18] $\beta \in$ [0, 1]. Given the $P_B \geq P_A$ constraint, we evaluate results for values of $P_A \leq P_B$. When $P_A < P_B$, we consider a difference between P_B and P_A ranging from: *i)* .01 to .1 with a .01 grid and *ii)* from .1 to .4 with a .1 grid.[19] Exactly as in the case of the ethical location *(a)* on the segment, we also introduce P_A^* according to *(4)*.

The following table shows the values of a and P_A yielding maximum profit in those cases in which socially responsible imitation is the most profitable outcome. In all cases β is always equal to unity, unless differently specified.

---

[16] Analytical details are available upon request.
[17] We define ethical neutrality the situation in which t = 1, since in this case the disutility of SR distance would be exactly equal to the difference between producer and consumer position on the segment in presence of linear costs of distance.
[18] a = 0.5 is the limit level of PMP imitation admitting an interior solution for the PMP optimal price.
[19] With values of $P_A \leq P_B$ $P_A = P_B - 0{,}4$ solutions were always dominated, given the values assigned to the exogenous values.

TABLE 1

VALUES OF THE PARAMETERS AND OF THE ENDOGENOUS VARIABLES YIELDING THE HIGHEST PROFIT
($\beta = 1$, unless differently specified)

	$c = 0.01$	$c = 0.02$	$c = 0.03$	$c = 0.04$	$c = 0.05$
$\bar{s} = 0.05$	$a = 0.381$ $P_A = 1.049$	$a = 0.310$ $P_A = 1.049^*$			
$\bar{s} = 0.06$	$a = 0.394$ $P_A = 1.059$	$a = 0.310$ $P_A = 1.059$ $a = 0.322$ $P_A = 1.058^{**}$			
$\bar{s} = 0.07$	$a = 0.402$ $P_A = 1.068$	$a = 0.330$ $P_A = 1.068$			
$\bar{s} = 0.08$	$a = 0.407$ $P_A = 1.078$	$a = 0.345$ $P_A = 1.078$			
$\bar{s} = 0.09$	$a = 0.410$ $P_A = 1.087$	$a = 0.355$ $P_A = 1.087$	$a = 0.308$ $P_A = 1.087^{**}$		
$\bar{s} = 0.1$	$a = 0.412$ $P_A = 1.097$	$a = 0.362$ $P_A = 1.097$	$a = 0.312$ $P_A = 1.097$		
$\bar{s} = 0.2$	$a = 0.4$ $P_A = 1.19$	$a = 0.375$ $P_A = 1.19$	$a = 0.35$ $P_A = 1.19$	$a = 0.325$ $P_A = 1.19$	
$\bar{s} = 0.3$	$a = 0.370$ $P_A = 1.277$	$a = 0.354$ $P_A = 1.277$	$a = 0.337$ $P_A = 1.277$	$a = 0.320$ $P_A = 1.277$	
$\bar{s} = 0.4$	$a = 0.337$ $P_A = 1.36$	$a = 0.325$ $P_A = 1.36$	$a = 0.312$ $P_A = 1.36$	$a = 0.3$ $P_A = 1.36$	$a = 0.287$ $P_A = 1.36$
$\bar{s} = 0.5$	$a = 0.302$ $P_A = 1.437$	$a = 0.297$ $P_A = 1.437$	$a = 0.282$ $P_A = 1.437$	$a = 0.272$ $P_A = 1.437$	
$\bar{s} = 0.6$	$a = 0.266$ $P_A = 1.51$	$a = 0.258$ $P_A = 1.51$	$a = 0.25$ $P_A = 1.51$		
$\bar{s} = 0.7$	$a = 0.230$ $P_A = 1.577$	$a = 0.223$ $P_A = 1.577$	$a = 0.216$ $P_A = 1.577$		
$\bar{s} = 0.8$	$a = 0.193$ $P_A = 1.64$	$a = 0.187$ $P_A = 1.64$			
$\bar{s} = 0.9$	$a = 0.156$ $P_A = 1.697$				
$\bar{s} = 1$	$a = 0.12$ $P_A = 1.75$				

* $\beta = 0.8$;
** $\beta = 0.9$.

Our main results can be summarized as follows:

SR imitation and full advertising effort are strict complements in the optimal PMP behaviour

For $\bar{s} \geq 0.1$ (closer to commodity market price minima), *ceteris paribus*, profit is always decreasing in β, with $a = 0$, and mostly increasing in β, with $a \neq 0$. Two possible values of β are found to be associated to maximum profit: $\beta = a = 0$ or $\beta = 1$ with $0.1 < a < 0.41$, depending on the values of $\bar{s}$ and c. These findings clearly show that, once the PMP finds it profitable to imitate, he will fully advertise it.

Complementarity between the PMP's optimal price and ethical location

It is no surprise that, as far as P_A is concerned, the optimal price is always increasing in $\bar{s}$ since a higher transfer implies higher levels for P_B, which, in turn, allow the PMP to charge profitably higher prices. Finally, P_A does not vary with "c" when $\beta = 1$. For smaller values of β P_A decreases, which is no surprise given *(4)*.

For a given value of the extra cost of SR advertising compatible with non zero PMP's SR imitation, the latter is inverse U-shaped with respect to the FT transfer.

Table 1 shows that the highest level of PMP imitation occurs in correspondence of intermediate values of $\bar{s}$. Imitation is lower when the FT transfer is the highest (commodity world price minima) because the marginal cost of imitation is high. It is also lower when FT transfer is lower (commodity world price maxima) because extra advertising costs are too high relative to the potential price increase available under ethical imitation. This depends on the dual effect of FT transfer on PMP's SR imitation discussed above (see *(5)*).

71

Consider as well that:

i) when we are close to commodity market price maxima ($\bar{s}$ slightly above 0.1) the optimal profit is increasing in β only with low marginal costs of advertising. As the $c/\bar{s}$ ratio increases, profits tend to be concave in β. Consequently, in this range of values, optimal profits can be associated with less than unit values of β.

ii) Under extreme world commodity market price downturns, ($\bar{s} = 1$), PMP's SR imitation is nonzero only with very low extra advertising costs of SR, respectively $c = 0.01$ and $c = 0.01/0.02$.

iii) Ceteris paribus, the optimal ethical content of the product decreases with c. Moreover, up to $\bar{s} = .4$, the threshold level of SR advertising costs which triggers PMP imitation is increasing in $\bar{s}$, because, the higher $\bar{s}$, the higher P_A and, as a result, *ceteris paribus*, the higher the extra expenditure in advertising the PMP can afford profitably. After that threshold, the cost effect dominates.

4. - The PMP Temptation of Misleading Advertising

4.1 *The PMP's Incentive to Cheat in a Static Framework*

In this version of the model the profit maximising producer is a monopolistic incumbent set at the extreme of the ethical segment (he chooses the strategy $a = 0$). An "orthodox" Fair Trader enters and places himself at $\bar{s}$. The PMP ethical location is not fixed and he can react in prices, ethical location and advertising effort of his SR choice. The incentive to cheat is defined as the difference between the PMP profit when he announces and advertises a given ethical stance, but does not transfer any margin of profit, and the PMP profit when advertising corresponds to effective ethical engagement.

Based on these assumptions we state the following proposition

PROPOSITION 2. If consumers cannot rely on independent sources of information on the PMP ethical product, the incentive to cheat is always positive.

We implicitly assumed so far that the information about the

ethical content of the product is truthful, *i.e.* it corresponds to the real transfer. We now turn to the case of cheating, *i.e.* the possibility that the producer misleadingly advertises an ethical content which does not correspond to the reality.

For the sake of simplicity we drop the hypothesis of an endogenous "*a*". We just assume that the PMP makes a product incorporating a given ethical content "*a*"[20] and faces the problem of choosing the price and the advertising investment.

His maximization problem is now

(9)
$$\max_{P_A,\beta} \pi = \left[P_A - w(1+a\bar{s}) - c\beta \right] \left(\sqrt{\frac{P_B - P_A}{t}} + a\beta \right)$$

s.t.: $a, \beta \in [0, 1]$, $P_A \in [w, P_B]$.
by arranging first order conditions we obtain the following values for interior solutions of optimal P_A and β:[21]

(10)
$$P_A^* = P_B - \frac{c^2}{4t_a^2}$$

(11)
$$\beta^* = \frac{w\bar{s}(1-a)}{2c} - \frac{3}{8}\frac{c}{t_a^2}$$

The inspection of *(10)* shows again the complementarity between PMP ethical imitation and prices since "*a*" is positively related to P_A. The optimal price is positively related to consumers costs of ethical distance since the latter raises marginal gains from imitation. The optimal price varies inversely with advertising costs because an increase in costs reduces the optimal SR advertising and therefore the impact of the ethical content of the product on the PMP's market share. The price non-negativity condition is met for

$$a \geq \frac{c}{2\sqrt{tw(1+\bar{s})}}$$

Inspection of *(11)* shows that ethical imitation and costs of

---

[20] We assume it without lack of generality since we are interested here in looking at the incentive to cheat for given levels of ethical imitation.
[21] Second order conditions for a maximum are met and are omitted for reasons of space.

SR advertising have a dual effect on optimal SR advertising. Indeed, β varies with a both positively — the higher the ethical content of the product, the higher the incentive to advertise it — and negatively — since a and β compete for the allocation of resources. The positive relationship between a and β is strengthened by "t" since, the higher the consumers' sensitiveness to ethical distance, the higher the gains from advertising ethical products. Furthermore, the positive effect of the PMP ethical stance on the transfer depends on the fact that, the higher the margin transferred, the lower is the relative cost of β with respect to a ($c/w\bar{s}$). The negative effect is generated by the fact that a and β compete on the side of costs.

Further inspection of parametric conditions ensuring interior solutions, described in *(10)* and *(11)*, show that an interior solution for β implies the following condition:

$$\frac{3}{4}\frac{c^2}{(1-a)a^2t} \le w\bar{s} \ge \frac{3}{4}\frac{c^2}{(1-a)a^2t} + \frac{2c}{1-a}$$

This is a rather restrictive condition. In fact, given the values of the parameters we assume, "$w\bar{s}$" tends to be higher than the upper condition. That is the case for most of the values considered in Table 1.[22] More specifically, with the exception of peaks of commodity market prices ($\bar{s} < .09$), the PMP will find it optimal to exert maximum advertising effort ($\beta = 1$).

We will therefore confine our analysis to this parametric region by assuming that the PMP will choose the $\beta = 1$ solution. The analysis for parametric regions which admit an interior solution for β (commodity market prices close to their historical peaks) is confined into an Appendix available upon request.

In the normal (no-cheating) case, the PMP profit is

$$(12) \qquad \pi^* = \frac{1}{2}\frac{w\bar{s}c}{t}\left(\frac{1}{a}-1\right) + w\bar{s}a(1-a) - \frac{1}{8}\frac{c^3}{a^3t^2} - \frac{3}{4}\frac{c^2}{at} - ac$$

This situation can be compared with the case of misleading

---

[22] Actually, the condition is met only for the following values: $\bar{s} = .05/c = .02$; $\bar{s} = .06/c = .02$ (for both values of a); $\bar{s} = .09/c = .03$.

advertising. Let's suppose that the PMP continues to announce and advertise the same ethical content as before, but this time without doing any SR imitation. In this (cheating) case, the PMP would choose β and P_A as to maximize the following:

$$(13) \qquad \pi_{ch} = (P_A - w - c\beta)\left(\sqrt{\frac{P_B - P_A}{t}} + \hat{a}\beta\right)$$

where $\hat{a}$ is the PMP announcement on the ethical content of the product.

Inspection of first order conditions shows that, in the cheating case, the PMP charges the same price than in the no-cheating case and advertises up to:

$$(14) \qquad \beta_{ch} = \frac{w\bar{s}}{2c} - \frac{3}{8}\frac{c}{t\hat{a}^2}$$

In presence of cheating, the optimal amount of advertising is bigger than in the no-cheating case, as there is no substitution effect between "a" and β. The β = 1 solution applies also when cheating occurs.

This implies that, in presence of cheating, profit is equal to:

$$(15) \qquad \pi_{ch} = \frac{1}{2}\frac{w\bar{s}c}{\hat{a}t} + w\bar{s}\hat{a} - \frac{1}{8}\frac{c^3}{\hat{a}^3 t^2} - \frac{3}{4}\frac{c^2}{\hat{a}t} - \hat{a}c$$

By assuming that the PMP announces an ethical content for his product which is equal to what he would have produced without cheating ($\hat{a} = a$), the two expressions can be compared.

Using *(12)* and *(15)*, and abstracting from intertemporal considerations, the incentive (*i.e.* the temptation) to cheat is then given by:

$$(16)^{23} \qquad T = E[\pi_{ch} - \pi^*] = w\bar{a}\bar{s}\left(\frac{1}{2}\frac{c}{at} + a\right)$$

---

[23] Indeed, we could ignore the difference between a and $\hat{a}$ in the two profit expressions. In this way those expressions which are similar in the two functions — except for the fact that they do depend on the effective ethical content of the product in one case and they depend on the announced ethical content in the other case — just cancel out. Indeed, those expressions refer to profit items which do not vary in the two cases: as long as the $a = \hat{a}$ equality holds, P_A and $[(P_B - P_A)/t]^{-1/2}$ are

where $wa\bar{s}$ are the cheater's unit gains in cost and the expression in parenthesis his market share if $\beta = 1$.

If the information provided by the PMP is the only source of knowledge for consumers, there is a positive incentive to false advertising on the part of the PMP. The incentive to cheat depends positively on the transfer, on consumers' sensitivity to ethical distance and on the marginal costs of extra-advertising. The effect of a is mainly positive but has also a negative component due to the complementarity between PMP price and ethical imitation.

4.2 *The Incentive to Cheat if Consumers can buy Information*

We now remove the hypothesis that consumers' have no information on the product other than the information provided by the PMP. More specifically, we assume that information is available on the market, at cost $I \in [1, \infty]$, where $I = 1$ is a normalization for the lowest cost of information.

According to the literature on deceptive advertising (Nelson, 1970, 1974) consumers' control on the quality/ specifications of the product, and hence on misleading advertising, varies whether the good in question is a "search good" ("experience good"), *i.e.* the quality of the product can be assessed before (only after) the purchase. In our case, the specification to be controlled by consumers is the existence and the real entity of the transfer (or the effective compliance to the announced socially responsible rules). In principle, we can suppose that consumers' control on those aspects of product quality can be carried out separately from actual consumption, even if costs of information can be high. This is because, even if most FT products can be typically considered as "experience goods" (for example "coffee", whose taste can be assessed only after trial), the SR characteristics of the products

---

the same both in the cheating and no-cheating situations. Furthermore, with regard to the impact of "a" on the market share, it does not make any difference whether the PMP is cheating, as long as he is not discovered. When the $\pi_{ch} - \pi^*$ difference is compared with the $\pi_0 - \pi_{ch}$ difference, it will make sense to distinguish the effective from the advertised ethical content of the product.

which are relevant here are of the search type (*i.e.* the share of profits which is actually transferred to producers). As a result, the only costs we do consider in the model are information costs. We do not take into account, for example, costs related to consumer's deception when they realize that the product they are actually consuming is not ethical, as it was possible for them to control quality before the purchase.

Taking into account the existence of information costs, we assume that only a fraction "q" of consumers chooses to be informed about the actual ethical content of the product, and that this fraction depends negatively on information costs. If information costs are high, the share of informed consumers will be low and *viceversa*. In particular, we assume a straight inverse relationship, *i.e.* $q = 1/I$, which implies $0 < q < 1$. Furthermore, for simplicity, we do not make any particular assumption on the ethical concern of informed consumers. Of course, consumers which are totally indifferent as to the ethical features of production will choose not to engage in any costly activity of information searching, so they will belong to the "non informed" group. More generally, consumers will choose to get informed as far as the costs of information will equal the psychological costs of buying non ethical products[24]. However, we can neglect the psychological reason for consumers' choice to buy information at this stage, the idea here being simply that, all other things being equal, the quantity of informed individuals will grow as the costs of information decrease, which will make cheating less profitable.

A different matter is how the informed consumers' would react once they discover the PMP cheating. In terms of our model, all things being equal, the PMP market share would shrink. Our assumption here is that informed consumers put no

---

[24] As a result, the group of informed people will include more ethical consumers than the group of uninformed. This difference would result in the two groups having a different average t, which, in turn, would imply that the incentive to cheat will depend also on the difference between the average sensitiveness to SR of the two groups. However, adding this further assumption to the model would not change much the results. The impact on the ethical preferences of consumers' will be discussed later, when the focus will be on their reaction to cheating.

stigma on the PMP producer when they realise he is cheating.[25] Consequently, once consumers acknowledge that the PMP's product is not ethical, the PMP's market share becomes function of the difference between P_B and P_A. In this case, the PMP profit would reduce to:

$$(17) \qquad \pi_0 = (P_A - w - c\beta_{ch})\left(\sqrt{\frac{P_B - P_A}{t}}\right)$$

where

$$(18) \qquad (\pi_0 - \pi_{ch}) = \hat{a}c - \hat{a}w\bar{s} + \frac{1}{4}\frac{c^2}{\hat{a}t}$$

These are the net gains from the a component of the market share the cheater has to give up once informed consumers verify that $a = 0$. If the unit price is bigger than the sum of unit costs ($P_A > w + c$), the whole expression is negative. The positive part of the expression refers to the negative component of price, according to (4).

In the cheating case, the PMP total profit will be the sum of the profit resulting from selling to the informed and to the uninformed consumers:

$$(19) \qquad \pi_{CH} = q\pi_0 + (1 - q)\,\pi_{ch}$$

However, this scenario represents the lower bound of informed consumers' reaction to the PMP deceptive behaviour.[26]

It is now possible to derive the incentive to cheat by comparing the PMP total profit in the cheating case with the PMP profit in the no cheating case for the "lower bound" (no

---

[25] Model solutions can be easily calculated under the hypothesis that informed consumers, in their product choice, apply some penalty to the PMP producer which is caught cheating.

[26] As a matter of fact, it may happen that, once consumers discover the PMP cheating, they react by reducing their demand for the PMP product even more than what envisaged by (17), for at least two reasons: i) if informed consumers have strong ethical preferences, they could decide to punish the PMP; ii) apart from their ethical preferences, consumers could regard cheating on the ethical characteristics of the product as a proxy for cheating on the quality of the product in general, in particular if the ethical good is of the experience type.

punishment) reaction of consumers. The condition for cheating is now the following:

$$(20) \qquad T = q\pi_0 + (1 - q) \pi_{ch} - \pi^*$$

which implies

$$T > 0 \text{ if } q < \frac{\pi_{ch} - \pi^*}{\pi_{ch} - \pi_0}$$

The temptation to cheat when consumers can buy information depends positively on net gains from cheating, as compared to the non cheating case, and negatively from those gains the cheater has to give up when he is discovered.

Taking into account *(15)* and *(16)* and simplifying, we obtain the following the condition for cheating:

$$(21) \qquad q < \frac{2\hat{a}w\bar{s}(c + 2a^2 t)}{4\hat{a}^2 t(w\bar{s} - c) - c^2}$$

This condition implies that, no matter how many informed consumers are in the market, if $4\hat{a}^2 tw\bar{s} < c (4\hat{a}^2 t - c)$, there will not be cheating. Such condition is likely to be met when the transfer is low.

On the contrary, if the $4\hat{a}^2 tw\bar{s} > c (4\hat{a}^2 t - c)$ condition is not met, cheating will occur. In particular, if the denominator is positive, so that the whole expression is positive, cheating will depend positively on a, as a bigger ethical content implies greater costs for the non-cheater, thereby increasing the gains from cheating. Under the same assumption, cheating will depend negatively on $\hat{a}$. Indeed, an increase in $\hat{a}$ enhances the cheater's market share, and, consequently the net gains he has to give up when he is discovered (both in the denominator). This impact is strengthened by the positive effect of $\hat{a}$ on price (nominator and both members of the denominator)[27]. Furthermore, cheating varies

---

[27] In fact, the positive effect of $\hat{a}$ on price (nominator) simplifies out for "$w\bar{s}$" and "c" (denominator), so that its net impact on temptation is negative, as it is divided by $- c$.

positively with "c", as an increase in c increases the market share[28] and also the non cheater's cost for ethical production (nominator). Moreover, as "c" increases, the price the cheater can charge decreases, while his total costs increase, as they are multiplied by a bigger market share. Both effects reduce the gains from cheating, and therefore the punishment if the cheater is discovered (denominator).

In order to see whether cheating is feasible for the range of values assumed so far in the model as "feasible", we calculated the quantity of information — as the share of informed consumers which is compatible with cheating for the values in Table 1. In particular, in all the cases in which ethical production and advertising are profitable, we found the threshold levels of q such that $T > 0$, *i.e.* the values of "q" after which cheating turns unprofitable. Our results are shown in Table 2:

TABLE 2

THRESHOLD LEVELS OF q FOR $T > 0$

	$c = 0.01$	$c = 0.02$	$c = 0.03$	$c = 0.04$	$c = 0.05$
$\bar{s} = 0.05$	$q = 0.4$	$q = 0.5$			
$\bar{s} = 0.06$	$q = 0.4$	$q = 0.5$			
$\bar{s} = 0.07$	$q = 0.4$	$q = 0.5$			
$\bar{s} = 0.08$	$q = 0.4$	$q = 0.5$			
$\bar{s} = 0.09$	$q = 0.4$	$q = 0.4$	$q = 0.5$		
$\bar{s} = 0.1$	$q = 0.4$	$q = 0.4$	$q = 0.5$		
$\bar{s} = 0.2$	$q = 0.4$	$q = 0.4$	$q = 0.4$	$q = 0.4$	
$\bar{s} = 0.3$	$q = 0.3$	$q = 0.4$	$q = 0.4$	$q = 0.4$	
$\bar{s} = 0.4$	$q = 0.3$	$q = 0.3$	$q = 0.3$	$q = 0.4$	$q = 0.4$
$\bar{s} = 0.5$	$q = 0.3$	$q = 0.3$	$q = 0.3$	$q = 0.3$	
$\bar{s} = 0.6$	$q = 0.2$	$q = 0.3$	$q = 0.3$		
$\bar{s} = 0.7$	$q = 0.2$	$q = 0.2$	$q = 0.3$		
$\bar{s} = 0.8$	$q = 0.2$	$q = 0.2$			
$\bar{s} = 0.9$	$q = 0.1$				
$\bar{s} = 1$	$q = 0.1$				

[28] This is because as c increases, P_A decreases, therefore the difference between P_B and P_A gets larger.

The maximum value of "q" necessary for cheating to be profitable when consumers can buy autonomous information is decreasing in $\bar{s}$ and increasing in "c". The upper values of the threshold are located on the upper side of the triangle, *i.e.* for higher $c/w\bar{s}$ ratios. This is no surprise, as we know from *(21)* that, as c increases, the temptation to cheat increases, *ceteris paribus*, which implies that cheating is profitable even for higher level of information in the market. Finally, the level of information necessary for consumers not to be cheated is very low in market downturn: with a share of informed consumers higher that 10%, cheating won't be profitable. In market upturn, that share increases up to 40-50%, depending on the marginal costs of extra advertising.

5. - Conclusions

In the traditional system of checks and balances of the pre-globalisation era the fight to inequality and the promotion of equal opportunities was essentially a "top-down" process, almost uniquely sustained by the action of domestic institutions and trade unions through the definition of a set of proper rules and fiscal incentives. In the post globalization era, the bottom-up action of concerned consumers and investors is playing a vicarious action to create new consensus for a new global governance which at the moment is still missing.

Such action could never be effective without the presence of a special kind of producers which we call "social market enterprises". These firms have an original not for profit approach and, by competing with standard profit maximizing firms, create interesting contagion effects.

We evaluate the effect of entry and development of this special kind of firms.

To do so we keep into account that asymmetric information is a crucial issue also in competition on social responsibility. It is indeed quite common to observe nowadays corporations advertising their ethical attitude and trying to overcome the skepticism of imperfectly informed consumers on the truthfulness of what is advertised.

In a situation in which demand for SR products grows, contagion effects are widespread and imitators have increasing market shares, the crucial issue is related to the capacity of consumers of perceiving the different ethical stance of "pioneers" and imitators in this market in spite of the strong informational asymmetry.

In this framework we provide some introductory analytical considerations on the issue by analyzing what changes in the competition between SR "pioneers" and profit maximizing imitators when we introduce the reasonable assumption that SR imitation needs to be advertised at some cost. An interesting finding is that, in relevant parametric regions, the introduction of advertising costs generates an inverse U-shaped relationship between PMP's SR imitation and the entity of the FT socially responsible transfer. This is because, if the pioneer's SR transfer is too high, the profit maximizing producer cannot afford costs of imitation, while, if the SR transfer is too low, fixed costs of advertising are too high relative to the potential price increase available to the PMP under ethical imitation.

Given the characteristics of our model which mimics the observed features of the competitive race between the PMP imitators and the FT (which applies a countercyclical premium on primary producers price) the implication of these results are that imitation will be discouraged symmetrically under extreme variations of commodity market prices.

Our work also investigates the incentive of the PMP to misleading advertising of his ethical stance. In this respect it shows that, if the information provided by the PMP is the only source of knowledge for consumers, there can be a positive incentive to false advertising on the part of the PMP. The incentive to cheat depends positively on the transfer, on consumers' sensitivity to ethical distance and on the marginal costs of extra-advertising. The effect of the degree of SR imitation on the incentive to cheat is mainly positive but has also a negative component, due to the complementarity between PMP price and ethical imitation.

BIBLIOGRAPHY

Adriani F. - Becchetti L., «Fair Trade: A "Third Generation Welfare" Mechanism to Make Globalisation Sustainable», *SSRN-CEIS, Working Paper*, n. 170, 2004.

Anderson S., «Spatial Competition and Price Leadership», *International Journal of Industrial Organization*, no. 5(4), 1987, pages 369-398.

Bahadur C. - Mendoza R., «Toward Free and Fair Trade: A Global Public Good Perspective», *Challenge*, no. 45, 2002, pages 21-62.

Basu K., «The Intriguing Relation between Minimum Adult Wage and Child Labour», *Economic Journal*, vol. 110, no. 462, March, 2000, pages 50-61.

Becchetti L. - Costantino M., «Fair Trade on Marginalized Producers: An Impact Analysis on Kenyan Farmers», *World Development*, vol. 36, no. 5, 2008, pages 823-842.

Becchetti L. - Giallonardo L. - Tessitore M.E., «On Ethical Product Differentiation with Asymmetric Linear Costs», *Rivista di Politica Economica*, forthcoming, 2007.

Becchetti L. - Rosati F., «Globalization and the Death of Distance in Social Preferences ad Inequity Aversion: Empirical Evidence from a Pilot Study on fair Trade Consumers», *The World Economy*, no. 30 (5), 2007, pages 807-830.

Becchetti L. - Solferino N., «On Ethical Product Differentiation», *Economia e Politica Industriale*, forthcoming, 2008.

Bhagwati J., *Fair Trade and Harmonization: Prerequisites for Free Trade?* Vol. 1: *Economic Analysis: Introduction*, Cambridge and London, MIT Press, 1996.

Cafedirect, *www.cafedirect.co.uk*, 21/8/03, 2003.

Cairncross F., *The Death of Distance*, London, Orion, 1997.

Camargo J., «Minimum Wage in Brazil: Theory, Policy and Empirical Evidence», Pontificia Universidade Catolica, *Discussion Paper*, no. 67, 1984.

Card D. - Krueger A.B., «Minimum Wages and Employment. A Case Study of the Fast Food Industry in West Virginia and in Pennsylvania», *American Economic Review*, no. 90(5), 2000, pages 1397-1420.

Carneiro F., «Salário Mínimo e Bem-Estar Social no Brasil: uma resenha da literatura», Rio de Janeiro, *IPEA, Texto para Discussão*, no. 880, 2002.

Corporate social responsibility monitor, *http://www.bsdglobal.com/issues/sr.asp*, 2003.

D'Aspremont C. - Gabsewicz J.J - Thisse J.F., «On Hotelling's Stability in Competition», *Econometrica*, no. 47, 1979, pages 114-1150.

Dasgupta P. - Maskin E., «The Existence of Equilibrium in Discontinuous Economic Games. II. Application», *Review of Economic Studies*, no. 53, 1986, pages 27-41.

De Benedictis L. - Helg R., «Globalizzazione», *Rivista di Politica Economica*, marzo-aprile, 2002.

Economides N., «Minimal and Maximal Product Differentiation in Hotelling's Duopoly», *Economic Letters*, no. 21, 1986, pages 67-71.

El-Hamidi F. - Terrell K., «The Impact of Minimum Wages on Wage Inequality and Employment in the Formal and Informal Sector in Costa Rica», Davidson Institute, *Working Paper*, no. 479, 2001.

Environics Research International, *2003*, Corporate social responsibility monitor, 2003.

EUROPEAN FAIR TRADE ASSOCIATION, *2001*, EFTA Yearbook, *www.eftafairtrade.org.*

——, *2003*, EFTA Report, *www.eftafairtrade.org.*

GIDDENS A., *Runaway World: How Globalization is Reshaping our Lives*, London, Routledge, 2000.

GONZAGA G. - MACHADO D., «Rendimento e Precos», in ABREU M. (ed.), *Estatisticas do Seculo XX*, Rio de Janeiro, IBGE, 2002.

HOTELLING H., «Stability in Competition», *Economic Journal*, no. 39, 1929, pages 41-57.

KIRZNER I.M., *Competition and Entrepreneurship*, The University of Chicago Press, Chicago and London, 1978.

LAMBERTINI L., «Unicity of Equilibrium in the Unconstrained Hotelling Model», *Regional Science and Urban Economics*, no. 27(6), 1997, pages 785-798.

LEMOS S., «The Effects of the Minimum Wage in the Formal and Informal Sectors in Brazil», University of Leicester and IZA Bonn, *Discussion Paper*, no. 1089, 2004.

MANNING A., «The Real Thin Theory: Monopsony in Modern Labour Markets», *Labour Economics*, no. 10, 2003, pages 105-134.

MASELAND R. - DE VAAL A., «How Fair is Fair Trade?», *De Economist*, no. 150(3), 2002, pages 251-272.

MOORE G., «The Fair Trade Movement: Parameters, Issues and Future Research», *Journal of Business Ethics*, no. 53, 2004, pages 1-2, 73-86.

NELSON PH., «Information and Consumer Behaviour», *Journal of Political Economy*, no. 78, 1970, pages 311-329.

——, «Advertising as Information», *Journal of Political Economy*, no. 82, 1974, pages 729-754.

ROBERTSON R., *Globalization*, Londra, Sage, 1992.

ROSS S.A., «Minimum Wages and the Card-Krueger Paradox», *Southern Economic Journal*, no. 67(2), 2000, pages 469-478.

SEN A., «Internal Consistency of Choice», *Econometrica*, no. 61, 1993, pages 495-521.

STIGLITZ J., *Globalization and its Discontents*, Publisher Information, New York and London, Norton Publication, 2002.

SURANOVIC S., «International Labour and Environmental Standards Agreements: Is This Fair Trade?», *The World Economy*, no. 25(2), 2002, pages 231-245.

VON HAYEK F.A., «The Use of Information in Society», *American Economic Review*, 1945.

WATERS M., *Globalisation*, New York, Rutgers, 2001.

ZAMAGNI S., *Complessità relazionale e comportamento economico, materiali per un nuovo paradigma della relazionalità*, Il Mulino, Bologna, 2002.

ZHOU D. - VERTINSKY I., «Strategic Location Decisions in a Growing Market», *Regional Science and Urban Economics*, no. 31, 2001, pages 523-533.

Should One Sell Domestic Firms to Foreign Ones? A Tale of Delegation, Acquisition and Collusion

Davide Dragone*

University of Bologna

In a model of repeated Cournot competition under complete information, I show how the existence of a fringe of managerial firms affects the stability of a cartel of strict profit-maximizing firms. There always exists a critical dimension of the fringe that makes the cartel unstable, and this dimension is non-monotone in the total number of firms. By appropriately selecting the dimension of the fringe, a policy maker can affect the equilibrium outcome. As an example, I consider the case of a domestic authority that is contemplating whether to allow entry of a fringe of managerial foreign firms in the domestic market to increase the competitive pressure, thereby enhancing domestic welfare. [JEL Classification: D43; L13; L21]

1. - Introduction

The issue of cartel stability has a long tradition. Several contributions have studied the factors and conditions affecting firms' ability to implement collusive practices over time, investigating, for example, the consequences of heterogeneity among agents (see, *inter alia*, d'Aspremont *et al.*, 1983; Donsimoni, 1985; Donsimoni *et al.*, 1986), the role of imperfect information (Green and Porter, 1984; Rothschild, 1999) and of product differentiation (Ross, 1992; Deneckere, 1983), the effect of the

* <*davide.dragone@unibo.it*>, Department of Economics. The Author thanks A. Mantovani, G.A. Minerva, C. Reggiani and the editor for useful comments. The usual disclaimer applies.

imposition of import quotas (Rotemberg and Saloner, 1986) or the consequences that fringes of non-colluding firms have on cartel stability (Shaffer, 1995).

The standard theoretical framework assumes profit-maximizing firms whose strategic variables are quantities and prices. Lambertini and Trombetta (2002) show that the stability of a cartel is also affected by strategic delegation. In a Cournot oligopoly, strategic delegation implies that owners delegate output decisions to managers whose objective functions differ from the owners'. When managerial incentives are a mix of profits and sales, managers behave aggressively and expand their output beyond the familiar Cournot Nash equilibrium. In the one-shot non-cooperative game, hiring managers is a dominant strategy in that delegation makes the firm more aggressive under Cournot competition and creates a credible commitment towards output expansion. In equilibrium output is larger and prices are lower as compared to the Cournot Nash equilibrium, thereby reducing profits and increasing consumer surplus (Fershtman, 1985; Vickers, 1985). Considering a repeated Cournot oligopoly between two firms, Lambertini and Trombetta (2002) show that delegation can make the cartel more unstable when owners collude in setting the incentives schemes, because it makes deviation from the cartel more appealing compared to a situation where firms are strict profit-seeking agents.

In the literature on cartel stability, much attention has been devoted to the stability of cartels of firms when there exists a competitive fringe (*inter alia*, d'Aspremont *et al.*, 1983; Donsimoni *et al.*, 1985; Donsimoni *et al.*, 1986; Thoron, 1998). Yet, if the number of firms in the industry is relatively small, the fringe firms do not necessarily behave as price-takers. Konishi and Lin (1999) and Shaffer (1995) consider an oligopoly where fringe firms make output decisions after the cartel has chosen its output level. In this paper, I adopt the same model as Vickers (1985) and Lambertini and Trombetta (2002), in which all output choices are taken simultaneously, and I extend the idea that delegation is a relevant strategic variable for cartel stability by considering how a cartel between owners of pure profit-seeking firms that

86

maximize joint profits is affected by a fringe of managerial firms. I show that it is always possible to make the cartel between owners unstable by appropriately selecting the dimension of the fringe, and that such a dimension is non-monotone in the total number of firms operating in the market.

I apply this set up to a situation where a domestic planner cares about consumer surplus and the profits of the domestic firms operating in the market. The planner must choose how many foreign managerial firms (which will constitute the fringe) she should allow to enter the domestic market through the acquisition of domestic firms. From the perspective of the domestic planner, I show that it is never optimal to allow the entry of foreign managerial firms when the market is very concentrated because the increase in output brought about by entry is not sufficiently counterbalanced by the reduction in profits accruing to the domestic firms. When the market is more fragmented and the incumbents are patient enough, it may be optimal to allow managerial firms to get in, as the competitive pressure exerted by entrants makes the cartel between domestic owners unstable, with the result that, after entry, all firms delegate and domestic welfare increases.

The remainder of the paper is organized as follows. Section 2 introduces the model. In Section 3, I study the optimal output choices made by managers once the incentive schemes are chosen by the owners of the firms. Depending on whether the domestic planner has allowed any entry and depending on the type of equilibrium outcome, four different cases can be distinguished. In Section 4, I separately study the four outcomes and determine the incentive schemes, the optimal output levels and the profits accruing to the domestic and foreign firms. In Section 5, I determine the optimal number of managerial firms that should be allowed in the market in case of entry. In Section 6, I compare the levels of domestic welfare associated to the four equilibria, and I determine the conditions that bring a domestic planner to choose whether and how many foreign firms should be let in the domestic market. Section 7 concludes.

2. - The Set Up

In an oligopolistic market, n firms compete in quantities for a homogeneous good whose inverse demand function is

$$(1) \qquad p = a - Q$$

where Q is total output and a is the reservation price. Under the assumption that production takes place at constant returns to scale, the profit function of each firm is the following:

$$(2) \qquad \pi = (p - c)q$$

where q is the output produced by the firm and c is the unit production cost, with $a > c \geq 0$.

The delegation game proposed by Vickers (1985) introduces for a firm's owner the option to delegate control of output decisions to a manager whose objective is

$$(3) \qquad \max_{q} M = \pi + \theta q$$

where parameter θ is a measure of the relevance of sales and is chosen by the owner of the firm to maximize profits. The incentive function in (3) is equivalent to assume that managers maximize a linear combination of profits and revenues, profits and costs, or sales and costs (d'Aspremont and Gerard-Varet, 1980; Fershtman, 1985; Fershtman and Judd, 1987; Katz, 1986; Sklivas, 1987). The special case $\theta = 0$ implies that the manager maximizes the same objective function as the owner would, and that there is no difference in the output levels produced by an entrepreneurial firm and a managerial one. In other words, $\theta = 0$ is equivalent to say that the owner hires no manager. In the remainder, I adopt the following:

ASSUMPTION 1. θ is non-negative.

In the non-cooperative subgame perfect equilibrium of the delegation game the non-negativity assumption on θ turns out to be non-binding (Vickers, 1985). Yet, when owners collude between them to maximize joint profits, the optimal amount of delegation is negative (Lambertini and Trombetta, 2002). Clearly, this is a conceivable outcome, but the empirical evidence points in the opposite direction, suggesting that managers do not place a negative weight on sales (Murphy, 1995; Baker *et* al., 1988).

Consider now the case in which *m* firms, which constitute the fringe of managerial firms, are allowed to enter the oligopolistic market according to the following:

ASSUMPTION 2. The number of firms in the market is constant over time.

This amounts to assume that no mergers are allowed for and that fringe firms can enter the market only through acquisition of $m \in [0, n]$ entrepreneurial incumbents. In the remainder of the paper, I will refer to the entrants as the "foreign firms" and to the incumbents as the "domestic firms". When $m = 0$, no foreign firm enters the market. Fringe firms are identical to the incumbents: owners are profit-maximizers and managers maximize a mix of profits and sales. The only difference is in the set of delegation options, as foreign firms are always managerial, while the incumbents have the option to be either managerial or strict profit-seekers.

The number of foreign entrants is regulated by a domestic social planner whose domestic social welfare function is given by the sum of the profits accruing to the domestic firms and consumer surplus:

$$(4) \qquad NSW(m) = (n - m)\pi_i + CS$$

where π_i is the individual profit of a domestic firm (*i* stands for incumbent) and *CS* is consumer surplus. The domestic planner chooses the dimension *m* of the fringe, taking into account the following game with complete and symmetric information:

Stage 1: The domestic planner allows *m* foreign managerial firms to buy *m* domestic firms.

Stage 2: Firms' owners simultaneously choose the incentive scheme of their manager.

Stage 3: Firm's managers simultaneously choose the output level.

When owners are simultaneously choosing whether to delegate or not, delegation is the dominant strategy of the one-shot noncooperative game (see, *inter alia*, Vickers, 1985; Basu, 1987; Fershtman and Judd, 1987; Sklivas, 1987; Fershtman, 1985; Katz, 1986). As this game is repeated infinitely many times, there is scope for stable forms of collusion. In this paper I focus on collusion occurring at stage 2, where the owners of the firms choose their organizational structure and determine the incentive scheme of their managers. To study the stability of these collusive agreements in front of a fringe of non-colluding firms (the "foreigners"), I assume the following:

ASSUMPTION 3. Foreign owners always delegate to managers.

The assumption above implies that only domestic owners have the option to collude by not delegating output choices to managers. The stability of the collusive agreement is assessed considering Friedman's grim trigger strategy (Friedman, 1971) in which players collude as long as all the others do so. After detecting a deviation by any of the participants to the cartel, all the cartel members revert to the non-cooperative equilibrium strategy (*i.e.* they set a positive θ) forever. Let $\delta \in [0, 1]$ be the intertemporal discount factor of the owner of a firm and adopt the following assumption:

ASSUMPTION 4. $\delta_i = \delta$ for all owners of domestic firms.

As the attention is focused only on the stability of the cartel between domestic owners, no specific assumption on the intertemporal discount factor of foreign owners and of domestic/foreign managers is needed[1].

3. - Output Choices

To solve the model, I proceed by backward induction

---

[1] Equivalently, we could assume that their discount factors are high enough to ensure that collusion is unstable; see LAMBERTINI L. - TROMBETTA M. (2002) for a complete analysis of cartel stability where both owners and managers collude.

considering the output choices that managers face at stage three, once the owners of the firms have chosen the amount of delegation $\theta \geq 0$ (where $\theta = 0$ is the limit case in which the manager is a pure profit-seeker or, equivalently, the owner hires no manager). Rewrite the objective function *(3)* of a manager with delegation θ_k, for all $k, j \in \{1,\ldots, n\}$ as follows:

$$(5) \qquad M_k = (a - c - \theta_k - \Sigma_{j \neq k} q_j - q_k) q_k$$

The first-order condition that firm k's manager considers in the market subgame is

$$(6) \qquad \frac{\partial M_k}{\partial q_k} = a - c - \theta_k - \Sigma_{j \neq k} q_j - 2q_k = 0$$

Solving for all managers yields the optimal quantity produced by each firm as a function of the delegation parameters chosen by the owners, the market structure and the production costs (Sklivas, 1987)[2]:

$$(7) \qquad q_k = \frac{a - c + n\theta_k - \Sigma_{j \neq k}\theta_j}{n+1}$$

The optimal output level of firm k is increasing in the amount of delegation chosen by its owner and decreasing in the delegation choices of the other firms. This implies the familiar result that, everything else equal, a managerial firm expands her output more than a profit-seeking firm (Vickers, 1985). Substituting and rearranging, total output and the profit accruing to each firm can be written as follows, respectively:

$$(8) \qquad Q = \frac{n(a-c) + \Sigma_{k=1}^{n}\theta_k}{1+n}$$

$$(9) \qquad \pi_k = \frac{(a-c-\theta_k - \Sigma_{j \neq k}\theta_j)(a-c+n\theta_k - \Sigma_{j \neq k}\theta_j)}{(n+1)^2}$$

---

[2] At this stage we do not need to specify whether the firm is managerial or profit-seeking, and the reaction functions of firm k's manager can be obtained without requiring symmetry.

The optimal amount of delegation of each manager k depends on the delegation choices of the owners of the remaining firms. As the delegation choices depend on whether the domestic social planner has allowed any domestic firm to enter the market (stage 1) *and* on the stability of the cartel between the domestic owners (at stage 2), four different outcomes can occur:

(i) no foreign firm is allowed to enter the market ($m = 0$) and the domestic owners set the incentive schemes non-cooperatively;

(ii) no foreign firm is allowed to enter the market ($m = 0$) and the domestic's owners collude;

(iii) $m \geq 1$ foreign firms enter the market and the domestic owners play non-cooperatively;

(iv) $m \geq 1$ foreign firms enter the market and the domestic owners collude.

For further reference, I will refer to the first outcome as the (D) equilibrium with no entry (where D stands for delegation), which corresponds to the solution of the delegation game by Vickers (1985) where all firms adopt symmetric managerial incentives and behave aggressively by expanding their output beyond the Cournot Nash quantities. In case *(ii)*, the owners optimally collude by not hiring managers, which implies that the delegation game reduces to a standard Cournot oligopoly with n identical firms. I will refer to the associated equilibrium as to the (C) outcome. In cases *(iii)* and *(iv)*, the domestic planner has allowed a fringe of managerial firms to enter the market. In case *(iii)* all domestic and foreign owners delegate; I will refer to it as the (D) outcome with entry. It is worth stressing that, given the symmetry between incumbents and entrants, the optimal amount of delegation, the individual production levels and profits are the same as those of case *(i)*. The only differences between case *(i)* and case *(iii)* concerns the level of domestic social welfare, that in case *(iii)* is clearly reduced by the profits accruing to the non-domestic firms. In case *(iv)* the domestic owners collude (by not hiring managers) and the foreigners constitute a fringe of managerial firms. As this case corresponds to a Stackelberg outcome, I will refer to it as the (S) outcome.

4. - Delegation Choices

In this Section, I consider the second stage of the game. I separately consider the four possible outcomes that can occur and determine the optimal incentive schemes, the corresponding output levels and individual profits. When collusion is profitable, I compute the critical value of the discount factor (which, in case of entry, also depends on the number of entrants) above which collusion is a stable outcome.

First, consider the cases where only domestic incumbents operate in the market. When $m = 0$ two possible equilibria can occur, depending on the intertemporal discount factor of the domestic owners, where either all of them delegate to managers or collude by not delegating.

4.1 (D) Outcome, m = 0

When all domestic owners $i, j \in \{1,..., n\}$ delegate to managers, the optimal amount of delegation is found solving the first-order condition $\delta\pi_i/\delta\theta_i = 0$, which yields (Vickers, 1985):

$$(10) \qquad \theta_i = \frac{(n-1)(a-c-\Sigma_{j\neq i}\theta_j)}{2n}$$

By imposing symmetry, the following optimal amount of delegation results:

$$(11) \qquad \theta_i^D = (a-c)\frac{(n-1)}{n^2+1} > 0$$

Substituting θ_i^D in the expressions (7)-(9), I get the following output levels and individual profits:

$$(12) \qquad q_i^D = (a-c)\frac{n}{n^2+1}$$

$$(13) \qquad Q^D = (a-c)\frac{n^2}{n^2+1}$$

$$(14) \qquad \pi_i^D = (a-c)^2\frac{n}{(1+n^2)^2}$$

4.2 (C) Outcome, m = 0

In case all domestic owners collude, they choose the delegation profile $\{\theta_1,..., \theta_n\}$ that maximizes the following joint profit function:

(15)
$$\Pi = \Sigma_{i=1}^{n}\pi_i$$
$$= \frac{1}{(n+1)^2}(a-c-\Sigma_{i=1}^{n}\theta_i)[n(a-c)+\Sigma_{i=1}^{n}\theta_i]$$

subject to the non-negativity condition on θ_i. Taking the derivative with respect to each θ_i yields:

(16)
$$\frac{\partial\Pi}{\partial\theta_i} = -\frac{1}{(n+1)^2}[(n-1)(a-c)+2\theta_i+2\Sigma_{i\neq j}\theta_i]$$

As $\theta \geq 0$, the partial derivative computed above is strictly negative, which implies that the optimal (corner) solution is $\theta_i = 0$ for all domestic owners[3]. In other words, when the domestic owners collude to maximize joint profits, the optimal choice is to hire no manager and behave as pure profit-maximizers. When this is the case, the following output levels and individual profits result:

(17)
$$q_i^C = (a-c)\frac{1}{n+1}$$

(18)
$$Q^C = (a-c)\frac{n}{n+1}$$

(19)
$$\pi_i^C = (a-c)^2 \frac{1}{(1+n)^2}$$

---

[3] If θ were unrestricted, the joint profit function (that is strictly concave because it is the sum of strictly concave functions) would be maximized when the following condition holds:

$$\Sigma_{i=1}^{n}\theta_i = -\frac{(n-1)(a-c)}{2} < 0$$

If the owners adopt symmetric incentive schemes, the optimal solution is

$$\theta_i = -\frac{(n-1)(a-c)}{2n}$$

that, for the case $n = 2$ simplifies to

$$\theta_i = -\frac{(a-c)}{4}$$

(see LAMBERTINI L. - TROMBETTA M., 2002).

94

Note that, compared with the (D) outcome, the Cournot Nash outcome is associated to a lower output. This implies higher individual profits but a lower level of consumer surplus, with the consequence that the level of social welfare associated to the (C) outcome is lower than the one associated with the (D) outcome with no entry.

To assess the conditions that make case (C) stable, I need to determine the deviation profits accruing to a domestic owner that does not set $\theta = 0$, while all the others do. Maximizing the profit function (9) with respect to θ_k the following reaction function obtains (Vickers, 1985):

$$(20) \qquad \theta_k = \frac{(n-1)(a-c-\Sigma_{j \neq k}\theta_j)}{2n} \text{ for } k,j \in \{1,...,n\}$$

If $\theta_j = 0$ for all $j \neq k$, the optimal deviation requires (Vickers, 1985):

$$(21) \qquad \theta_d(0) = \frac{(a-c)(n-1)}{2n}$$

where the zero in brackets signals this is the case of no entry and the pedix 'd' stands for defection. The corresponding deviation profit is

$$(22) \qquad \pi_d(0) = \frac{(a-c)^2}{4n} > \pi^C$$

By considering trigger strategies, collusion between domestic owners is stable if

$$(23) \qquad \delta > \delta^*(n,0) = \frac{\pi_d(0) - \pi^C}{\pi_d(0) - \pi^D} = \frac{\left(1+n^2\right)^2}{\left(1+n\right)^4}$$

(see Lambertini and Trombetta, 2002), where π^C and π^D are, respectively, the profits accruing to the owner of the domestic firm in the collusive and in the delegating equilibrium with no entry. The zero appearing in brackets signals this is the case where $m = 0$.

4.3 (D) Outcome, $m \geq 1$

Now consider the case where $m \in \{1,..., n\}$ managerial foreign firms have entered the market. As entrants and incumbents face the same technology and the good is homogeneous, the only difference between them is that the incumbents have the option to collude. Clearly, when they all delegate this difference is lost and the same θ's, output levels, individual profits and consumer surplus as in the (D) case with no entry obtains. All equilibrium outcomes only depend on fixed parameters such as the reservation price, the unit cost of production and the total number of firms in the market. Hence, the number of entrants m is relevant only to compute the level of domestic social welfare.

4.4 (S) Outcome, $m \geq 1$

Consider now the case in which the domestic planner has allowed $m \in \{1,..., n\}$ managerial firms to buy m incumbents and the remaining $n - m$ incumbents collude by choosing the profile of delegation that maximizes joint profits. Before proceeding note that the (S) outcome requires m to lie in the interval $[1, n - 2]$, with $n \geq 3$. The lower bound is necessary because we are in the case in which entry occurs, the upper bound because the domestic firms must be at least two to collude.

I proceed by first assessing the maximum number of entrants that makes collusion between domestic owners profitable; then I determine the conditions for cartel stability. With reference to trigger strategies, stability can be assessed in terms of the critical value of the intertemporal discount factor that makes collusion stable. Equivalently, the same condition can be expressed as a function of the dimension of the fringe. The advantage of the latter condition is that, given n and δ, it informs about the critical dimension of the fringe that makes the cartel between domestic incumbents unstable. This implies that the domestic social planner can influence the equilibrium outcome by appropriately choosing the dimension of the fringe.

For expositional convenience, let the entrants be indicated by $e, f \in \{1,\ldots, m\}$ and the incumbents by $i \in \{m + 1,\ldots, n\}$. Consider first the delegation choices made by the foreign owners. They choose non-cooperatively the optimal amount of delegation that maximizes the objective function in *(9)*, that can be written as follows:

$$(24) \quad \pi_e = \frac{(a-c-\theta_e - \Sigma_{f \neq e}\theta_f - \Sigma_{i=m+1}^{n}\theta_i)(a-c+n\theta_e - \Sigma_{f \neq e}\theta_f - \Sigma_{i=m+1}^{n}\theta_i)}{(n+1)^2}$$

The associated first-order condition is:

$$(25) \quad \frac{\partial \pi_e}{\partial \theta_e} = \frac{1}{(n+1)^2}[(n-1)(a-c)-2n\theta_e +(n-1)\Sigma_{f \neq e}\theta_f +(n-1)\Sigma_{i=m+1}^{n}\theta_i]$$

Now consider the domestic owners. They choose the profile that maximizes the following joint profit function:

$$(26) \quad \begin{aligned} \Pi &= \Sigma_{i=1}^{n-m}\pi_i \\ &= \frac{1}{(n+1)^2}(a-c-\Sigma_{i=m+1}^{n}\theta_i - \Sigma_{e=1}^{m}\theta_e) \\ &\quad [(n-m)(a-c)+(m+1)\Sigma_{i=m+1}^{n}\theta_i -(n-m)\Sigma_{e=1}^{m}\theta_e] \end{aligned}$$

To find the optimal solution, rewrite equation *(26)* as

$$(27) \quad \begin{aligned} \Pi &= \frac{1}{(n+1)^2}(a-c-\theta_{m+1} - \Sigma_{i=m+2}^{n}\theta_i - \Sigma_{e=1}^{m}\theta_e) \\ &\quad [(n-m)(a-c)+(m+1)\theta_{m+1} +(m+1)\Sigma_{i=m+2}^{n}\theta_i -(n-m)\Sigma_{e=1}^{m}\theta_e] \end{aligned}$$

where θ_{m+1} is the amount of delegation chosen by one of the domestic owners. The partial derivative of the joint profit function with respect to θ_{m+1} yields:

$$(28) \quad \begin{aligned} \frac{\partial \Pi}{\partial \theta_{m+1}} &= \frac{1}{(n+1)^2}[(1+2m-n)(a-c)-2(1+m)(\theta_{m+1} + \Sigma_{i=m+2}^{n}\theta_i)+ \\ &\quad -(1+2m-n)\Sigma_{e=1}^{m}\theta_e] \end{aligned}$$

I now assume that the domestic owners adopt a symmetric solution, so that $\theta_{m+1} = \ldots = \theta_n = \theta_i^S$, where the apex S stands for Stackelberg outcome. Note also that, as all foreign owners are identical, in equilibrium they adopt a symmetric solution $\theta_e = \theta_f = \theta_e^S$ for all $e, f \in \{1,..., m\}$. This allows to simplify the first-order conditions *(25)* and *(28)* as follows

(29) $\quad \dfrac{\partial \pi_e}{\partial \theta_e} = \dfrac{1}{(n+1)^2}[(n-1)(a-c)-(nm+n-m+1)\theta_e^S - (n^2 - nm - n + m)\theta_i^S]$

(30) $\quad \dfrac{\partial \Pi}{\partial \theta_i} = \dfrac{1}{(n+1)^2}[(a-c)(1+2m-n)-2(n-m)(1+m)\theta_i^S - m(1+2m-n)\theta_e^S]$

When

$$m < \frac{n-1}{2}$$

the partial derivative of the joint profit function *(30)* is negative and, as in the case of collusion with no entry considered in the previous section, the non-negativity restriction implies that the optimal choice of the $n - m$ domestic owners is to set $\theta_i^S = 0$ for all $i \in \{1,..., n - m\}$[4]. Accordingly, the m foreign owners choose the optimal amount of delegation that solves the following condition

(31) $\quad \dfrac{\partial \pi_e}{\partial \theta_e} = \dfrac{1}{(n+1)^2}[(n-1)(a-c)-2n\theta_e^S + (n-1)\Sigma_{e \neq f}\theta_f^S]=0$

where $e, f \in \{1,..., m\}$. Exploiting symmetry, the optimal amount of delegation for the foreign entrants is:

(32) $$\theta_e^S = (a-c)\frac{n-1}{n-m+nm+1}$$

Substituting θ_e^S in the reaction function of the managers *(7)* and rearranging I obtain the output levels of the domestic entrants and the foreign incumbents, respectively:

(33) $$q_e^S(m) = (a-c)\frac{n}{n-m+nm+1}$$

---

[4] The Appendix contains the computations showing that, with $m \geq (n-1)/2$, collusion between incumbents is never profitable.

$$(34) \qquad q_i^S(m) = (a-c)\frac{1}{n-m+nm+1}$$

where m signals that these outcomes depend on the number of entrants. The associated total output levels and individual profits are, respectively,

$$(35) \qquad Q^S(m) = (a-c)\frac{nm+n-m}{n+nm-m+1}$$

$$(36) \qquad \pi_e^S(m) = (a-c)^2 \frac{n}{(n-m+nm+1)^2}$$

$$(37) \qquad \pi_i^S(m) = (a-c)^2 \frac{1}{(n-m+nm+1)^2}$$

Comparing $\pi_i^S(m)$ with π_i^D to check when collusion between incumbents is profitable yields:

$$(38) \quad \pi_i^S(m) - \pi_i^D = (a-c)^2 \frac{(n-1)(n^3 - n^2 m^2 - 2n^2 m + m^2 n - 2mn - 1)}{(1+n^2)^2(n-m+nm+1)^2}$$

This expression is positive when $m \in (m_1, m_2)$, where

$$m_{1,2} = \frac{-n^2 - n \pm (1+n^2)\sqrt{n}}{n(n-1)}$$

I disregard the negative solution and note that

$$m_2 = \frac{-n^2 - n + (1+n^2)\sqrt{n}}{n(n-1)} \geq 1$$

if $n > 3.38$.

PROPOSITION 1. In case of entry, collusion between the domestic owners is profitable if $n \geq 4$ and $m \in [1, m_2]$.

When the market is very concentrated, if there is at least on managerial firm in the market it is never profitable to be pure profit-seekers. This occurs because the profits accruing to the profit-seeking firms are lower than those associated to a (D) outcome, in which all firms are managerial.

REMARK 2 If $n = 3$ and $m = 1$, collusion between domestic owners is never profitable.

PROPOSITION 3. When collusion between domestic owners is profitable after entry, the entrants optimally set

$$\theta_e^S = (a-c)\frac{n-1}{n-m+nm+1}$$

for all $e \in \{1,..., m\}$ and the incumbents set $\theta_i^S = 0$ for all $i \in \{m + 1,..., n\}$.

After determining when the cartel is profitable, I want to assess the stability of the cartel between domestic owners. When all foreign owners set the amount of delegation according to *(32)* and all but one domestic owners set $\theta_i^S = 0$, the optimal delegation of the domestic owner that deviates from the cartel is:

(39)
$$\theta_d(m) = (a-c)\frac{n^2-1}{2n(n-m+nm+1)}$$

which entails the following deviation profit:

(40)
$$\pi_d(m) = (a-c)^2 \frac{(1+n^2)}{4n(n-m+nm+1)^2} > \pi_i^S(m)$$

By considering trigger strategies, collusion between domestic owners is stable if

(41)
$$\delta > \delta^*(n,m) = \frac{\pi_d(m)-\pi_i^S(m)}{\pi_d(m)-\pi^D}$$

where the critical value of the discount function is given by the following expression:

(42)
$$\delta^*(n,m) = \frac{(n-1)(1+n^2)^2}{(n^2-1-2nm)(n^3+2n^2m-2nm+3n^2+3n+1)}$$

PROPOSITION 4. If $n \geq 4$ and $m \in [1, m_2]$ collusion between domestic owners is stable if $\delta > \delta^*(n, m)$.

In Graph 1 the curves $\delta^*(n, 0)$, $\delta^*(n, 1)$ and $\delta^*(n, 2)$ are drawn to illustrate how the stability of the (S) outcome depends

GRAPH 1

CRITICAL VALUE OF THE DISCOUNT RATE ABOVE WHICH
COLLUSION BETWEEN NATIONAL OWNERS IS STABLE. THE
CURVES CORRESPOND, FROM BOTTOM TO TOP, TO
$m=0$, $m=1$ and $m=2$

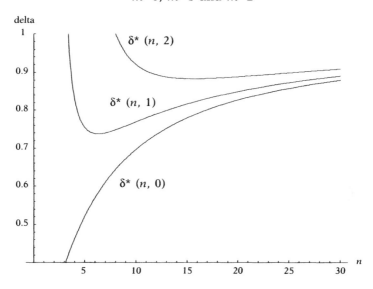

on δ and n. For $\delta < \delta^*$ $(n, 0)$ the (D) outcome always obtains, even
when there is no entrant, because the domestic owners are too
impatient to collude successfully. Between δ^* $(n, 0)$ and δ^* $(n, 1)$,
the (C) outcome obtains if there is no entry, and the (D) outcome
obtains when there is at least one entrant. Between the curves
δ^* $(n, 1)$ and δ^* $(n, 2)$, the (C) outcome emerges before entry
(because $\delta > \delta^*$ $(n, 0)$), and the (S) outcome is stable if there is one
entrant, but unstable if there are two entrants (because (n, δ) is
such that δ^* $(n, 1) < \delta < \delta^*$ $(n, 2)$).

For $m \geq 1$, δ^* (n, m) is non monotone in n: it is decreasing for
low values of n and it is increasing when n is large (see also
Lambertini and Trombetta, 2002). Intuitively a stable cartel needs
high discount rates when the total number of firms is low because
$\pi_d(m) - \pi_i^S(m)$, the incentive to deviate from the cartel, is high. As
n increases, the gains from deviation decrease, while $\pi_d(m) - \pi^D$,
the difference between the one-period profit from deviation and the

punishment profit, grows rapidly. This makes collusion more and more appealing, and lower discount rates are required. If n increases further, all profits decrease, but the gains from collusion decrease more rapidly than the punishment profits π^D corresponding to the non-cooperative solution. This makes the cartel more unstable, and higher discount rates are required to sustain collusion.

With reference to condition *(41)*, stability can also be assessed in terms of the critical number of firms that makes collusion between foreign owners stable. Let m^* (n, δ) be such a number, which is defined as

$$(43) \quad m^*(n,\delta) = Max\{\frac{-2\delta n(n+1)+(1+n^2)\sqrt{\delta[\delta(n^2+1)-(n^2-1)]}}{2\delta(n-1)n},1\} < m_2$$

In Graph 2 the critical dimension of the fringe of managerial firms that makes the cartel between domestic owners unstable is

GRAPH 2

PLOT OF THE CRITICAL DIMENSION OF THE FRINGE ENSURING
STABILITY TO THE CARTEL BETWEEN NATIONAL OWNERS.
GIVEN (n, δ), THE CARTEL IS UNSTABLE
IF $m > m^*$ (n, δ) AND STABLE OTHERWISE

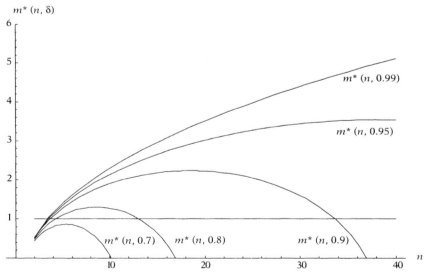

drawn for $n \geq 4$. The horizontal line corresponds to $m = 1$. For increasing values of δ, the m^* locus shifts upward, implying that, *ceteris paribus*, a larger fringe is needed to make the cartel unstable. Note that $m^* \geq 1$ if $\delta \geq \delta^* (n, 1)$, which means that one entrant can make the (S) outcome stable if the domestic owners are patient enough, given the total number of firms, to sustain collusion.

PROPOSITION 5. For $n \geq 4$:
– there exists a unique critical dimension of the fringe $m^* (n, \delta)$ such that, after entry of foreign managerial firms, collusion between owners is unstable if $m > m^* (n, \delta)$
– if $\delta > \delta^* (n, 1)$, then $m^* (n, \delta) > 1$ is a non-monotone, strictly concave function of n
– if $\delta < \delta^* (n, 1)$ or, equivalently, $m^* (n, \delta) < 1$, one entrant is enough to make the (S) outcome unstable

5. - Optimal Number of Entrants

Considering the welfare function of a domestic social planner, I now determine the number of entrants that maximizes the level of domestic welfare associated with the (D) outcome with $m \geq 1$ entrants and the (S) outcome with $m \geq 1$ entrants. Using the the results of the previous section, the levels of domestic social welfare are, respectively:

(44)
$$NSW^D(m) = (a-c)^2 \frac{n\left(n^3 + 2n - 2m\right)}{2\left(n^2 + 1\right)^2}$$
$$\text{if } m \in [\min\{m^*(n,\delta),1\}, n]$$

(45)
$$NSW^S(m) = \frac{(a-c)^2}{(n+nm-m+1)^2}[n-m+\frac{1}{2}(n+nm-m)^2]$$
$$\text{if } n \geq 4 \text{ and } m \in [1, m^*(n,\delta))$$

REMARK 6. $NWS^D(m)$ is decreasing in $NWS^S(m)$ is increasing in m.

The level of *NWS* associated to the (D) equilibrium is decreasing in the number of entrants because the output does not depend on the number of entrants, but total profits do so. On the other hand, the level of social welfare associated to the (S) outcome increases with m because the gains on consumer surplus (due to the aggressive output choices of the m managerial firms) more than compensate for the losses in the domestic profits. Given the previous remark, the optimal choice of the domestic planner would be to choose m^* given n and δ, in both cases. Yet, there exists an implicit constraint, in that m must be an integer number. Let m_s = *floor* $(m^*(n, \delta))$ be the integer part of $m^*(n, \delta)$ and m_D = *ceiling* $m^*(n, \delta))$[5]. For each outcome, the optimal number of firms is as follows:

PROPOSITION 7. When collusion after entry is not stable and the (D) outcome obtains, domestic social welfare is maximum if $m = m_D$.

PROPOSITION 8. When collusion after entry is stable and the (S) outcome obtains, domestic social welfare is maximum if $m = m_S$.

6. - Equilibrium Selection

The levels of *NWS* for the (D) equilibrium with no entry, the (C) equilibrium with no entry, the (D) equilibrium with m_D entrants and the (S) equilibrium with m_S entrants are, respectively:

$$(46) \qquad NSW^D(0) = (a-c)^2 \frac{n^2(n^2+2)}{2(n^2+1)^2}$$

---

[5] The floor and the ceiling functions are two functions which convert arbitrary real numbers to close integers. The floor function of a real number x is a function that returns the highest integer less than or equal to x. Formally, for all real numbers x, *floor* (x) = max $\{n \in Z | n \le x\}$. The ceiling function is the function that returns the smallest integer not less than x, or, formally, *ceiling* (x) = min $\{n \in Z | x \le n\}$.

(47)
$$NSW^C = (a-c)^2 \frac{n(n+2)}{2(n+1)^2}$$

(48)
$$NSW^D(m_D) = (a-c)^2 \frac{n(n^3+2n-2m_D)}{2(n^2+1)^2}$$

(49)
$$NSW^S(m_S) = (a-c)^2 \frac{[n-m+\frac{1}{2}(n+nm_S-m_S)^2]}{(n+nm_S-m_S+1)^2}$$

It is easy to check that the (D) outcome with no entry is associated to the highest level of domestic welfare where all firms are domestics and managerial. This outcome corresponds to the more competitive of the four cases, and it occurs when $\delta < \delta^*$. The (S) outcome with m_S entrants yields the lowest domestic welfare and is not desirable. The social planner will try to avoid it either by not allowing any foreign firm to enter the market or by allowing m_D foreign firms to enter and make the (S) outcome unstable. In the former case, a (D) outcome with no entry or a (C) outcome obtains, while in the latter a (D) outcome with m_D entrants obtains. As the (D) outcome with no entry is the most desirable outcome, no policy intervention is needed when $\delta < \delta^*$. On the contrary, when $\delta > \delta^*$ it is optimal for the domestic planner to allow m_D entrants in the market if $NWS^D(m_D) > NWS^C$.

PROPOSITION 9. No foreign firm should be allowed to enter the market:
- if $\delta < \delta^*$ $(n, 0)$,
- if $n \in \{2, 3\}$,
- if $\delta > \delta^*$ $(n, 1)$ and $NWS^C > NWS^D(m_D)$.

PROPOSITION 10. It is optimal to allow m_D foreign firms to enter the market
- if $\delta \in (\delta^*, \delta^*(n, 1))$ and $n > 3$
- if $\delta > \delta^*$ $(n, 1)$ and $NWS^C < NWS^D(m_D)$.

The propositions determine the conditions that should drive the decision of the domestic planner. To understand the logic, observe that if $\delta < \delta^*$ $(n, 0)$, the (D) outcome with no entrants obtains. This is the equilibrium with the highest domestic welfare level, and thus no intervention is needed. If $\delta > \delta^*$ $(n, 0)$ we must distinguish different cases by comparing NWS^C (which occurs when $m = 0$ and $\delta > \delta^*$) and $NWS^D(m_D)$ (which occurs when $m = m_D \geq 1$).

Case (a): $n \in \{2, 3\}$. In this case the (C) outcome obtains before entry and the (D) outcome with $m \in \{1, 2, 3\}$ entrants. As $NWS^C > NWS^D(m)$ if $n < 3.28$, no intervention is needed.

Case (b): $n > 3$ and $\delta \in (\delta^*, \delta^* (n, 1))$. In this case, before entry the (C) outcome obtains and, in case $m_D = 1$, the (D) outcome with one entrant obtains. It is optimal to allow one managerial firm to enter the market because $NWS^C < NWS^D(1)$ for all n: entry is desirable because it improves the economy by inducing a (D) equilibrium that is better than the (C) outcome.

Case (c): $\delta > \delta^* (n, 1)$. As for the previous case, the (C) outcome results before entry and the (D) outcome with $m_D \geq 2$ entrants results after entry. With respect to the previous case, note that m_D changes as a function of n and δ and the levels of domestic welfare must be explicitly computed and compared. To illustrate this point, in Graph 3 I set $\delta = .85$ and I plot both m^* and m_D as functions of n. The jumps occur at $n = 3.88$ (where m_D becomes 2) and at $n = 20.13$ (where m_D comes back to one). In Graph 4 I plot both $NWS^D(m_D)$ and NWS^C to show graphically the relative rankings as functions of n. Now consider a market where $n = 4$. We are in case (c) because $\delta = .85 > \delta^* (n, 1) = .83$. With this configuration, $m^*(n, \delta) = 1.02$ and $m_D = 2$. The comparison between the two associated levels of domestic welfare yields $NWS^C = .48 > NWS^D(2) = .47$, and it is optimal to let no entrant in. If instead $n = 6$, m_D would still be 2, but we would get the opposite ranking as $NWS^C = .489 < NWS^D(2) = .49$. In this case, the (C) outcome is better than the (D) outcome with m_D entrants and no intervention is needed.

GRAPH 3

PLOT OF $m^*(n, \delta)$ AND m_D AS FUNCTIONS OF n

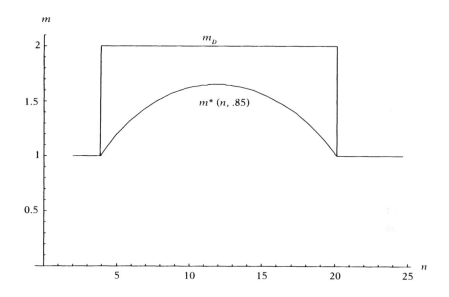

GRAPH 4

COMPARISON OF THE LEVELS OF NATIONAL WELFARE FOR THE
(C) OUTCOME (THICK CURVE) AND THE (D) OUTCOME WITH m_D
ENTRANTS WHEN $\delta = 0.85$

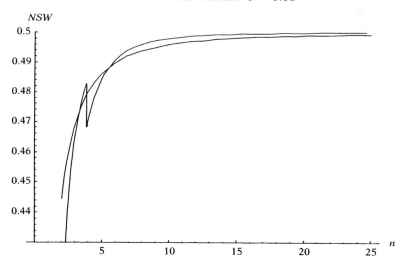

7. - Conclusion

The separation between ownership and control of market decisions significantly affects the competitive behaviour of an oligopolist. In a Cournot oligopoly, when the incentive schemes of the managers are a mix of profits and sales, managers optimally behave aggressively by expanding their output. As this outcome is dominated by the Cournot Nash equilibrium, the owners of the firms might collude to reduce competition. I have investigated how a cartel between owners is affected by the existence of a fringe of firms that always delegate output choices to managers. Adopting the Vickers (1985) framework, I have shown that it is always possible to make unstable the cartel between owners by appropriately selecting the dimension of the fringe, and that the dimension of the fringe that ensures cartel stability is non-monotone in the total number of firms operating in the market.

The introduction of a fringe of managerial firms can be used by a planner in order to modify the equilibrium outcome. For example, a domestic planner might contemplate whether to allow foreign managerial firms to enter a domestic market where the owners of firms collude by adopting organizational structures that reduce competition.

To show that collusion between incumbents is not profitable when

$$m > \frac{n-1}{2}$$

consider profit functions *(29)* and *(30)*. If

$$m > \frac{n-1}{2}$$

the optimal amount of delegation of domestic and foreign managers is as follows:

$$\hat{\theta}_e = (a-c)\frac{n-1}{2+m+nm}$$

$$\hat{\theta}_i = (a-c)\frac{1+2m-n}{(2+m+nm)(n-m)}$$

Note that all owners always choose a positive amount of delegation. Substituting $\hat{\theta}_e$ and $\hat{\theta}_i$ in the manager's reaction functions *(7)* and rearranging, I obtain the output levels of, respectively, the domestic entrants and the foreign incumbents:

$$\hat{q}_e(m) = (a-c)\frac{n}{2+m+nm}$$

$$\hat{q}_i(m) = (a-c)\frac{1+m}{(n-m)(2+m+nm)}$$

where m in brackets signals that these outcomes depend on the number of entrants. The associated total output levels and individual profits are, respectively:

$$\hat{Q}(m) = (a-c)\frac{(1+m+mn)}{2+m+nm}$$

$$\hat{\pi}_e(m) = (a-c)^2 \frac{n}{(1+nm-m+n)^2}$$

$$\hat{\pi}_i(m) = (a-c)^2 \frac{1}{(1+nm-m+n)^2}$$

We are now ready to check whether collusion between domestic owners is profitable. Comparing $\hat{\pi}_i(m)$ and π_i^D yields:

$$\hat{\pi}_i(m) - \pi_i^D = -(a-c)^2 \frac{(1+n)(n-m-1)(1+3nm+m^2n-n^2-mn^2+m^2n)}{(n-m)(2+m+nm)^2(1+n^2)^2}$$

As all the terms in brackets are positive, the cartel is never profitable.

BIBLIOGRAPHY

BASU K., «Stackelberg Equilibrium in Oligopoly: An Explanation based on Managerial Incentives», *Economics Letters*, no. 49, 1995, pages 459-464.

D'ASPREMONT C. - JACQUEMIN A. - GABSZEWICZ J.J. - WEYMARK J., «On the Stability of Collusive Price Leadership», *Canadian Journal of Economics*, no. 16, 1983, pages 17-25.

DENECKERE R., «Duopoly Supergames with Product Differentiation», *Economics Letters*, no. 11, 1983, pages 37-42.

DONSIMONI M.P., «Stable Heterogeneous Cartels», *Interdomestic Journal of Industrial Organisation*, no. 3, 1985, pages 451-467.

DONSIMONI M.P. - ECONOMIDES N. - POLEMARCHAKIS H., «Stable Cartels», *Interdomestic Economic Review*, no. 27, 1986, pages 317-327.

ESCRIHUELA-VILLAR M., «Cartel Sustainability and Cartel Stability», *Working Papers*, no. 2004.44, Fondazione Eni Enrico Mattei, 2004.

FERSHTMAN C., «Internal Organisations and Managerial Incentives as Strategic Variables in a Competitive Environment», *Interdomestic Journal of Industrial Organisation*, no. 3, 1985, pages 245-253.

FERSHTMAN C. - JUDD K., «Equilibrium Incentives in Oligopoly», *American Economic Review*, no. 77, 1987, pages 927-940.

FERSHTMAN C. - JUDD K. - KALAI E., «Observable Contracts: Strategic Delegation and Cooperation», *Interdomestic Economic Review*, no. 32, 1991, pages 551-559.

FRIEDMAN J.W., «A Non-Cooperative Equilibrium for Supergames», *Review of Economic Studies*, no. 38, 1971, pages 1-12.

GREEN E.J. - PORTER R.H., «Noncooperative Collusion under Imperfect Price Information», *Econometrica*, no. 52, 1984, pages 87-100.

KATZ M.L., «Game-Playing Agents: Unobservable Contracts as Precommitments», *The RAND Journal of Economics*, no. 22, 1991, pages 307-328.

KONISHI H. - LIN P., «Stable Cartels with a Cournot Fringe in a Symmetric Oligopoly», *Keio Economics Studies*, no. 36, 1999, pages 1-10.

LAMBERTINI L. - TROMBETTA M., «Delegation and Firms' Ability to Collude», *Journal of Economic Behaviour and Organization*, no. 47, 2002, pages 359-373.

ROSS T.W., «Cartel Stability and Product Differentiation», *Interdomestic Journal of Industrial Organization*, no. 10, 1992, pages 1-13.

ROTEMBERG J. - SALONER G., «A Supergame-Theoretic Model of Business Cycle and Price Wars during Booms», *American Economic Review*, no. 76, 1986, pages 390-407.

ROTHSCHILD R., «Cartel Stability when Costs are Heterogeneous», *Interdomestic Journal of Industrial Organization*, no. 17, 1999, pages 717-734.

SHAFFER S., «Stable Cartels with a Cournot Fringe», *Southern Economic Journal*, no. 61, 1985.

SKLIVAS S.D., «The Strategic Choice of Managerial Incentives», *The RAND Journal of Economics*, no. 18, 1987, pages 452-458.

THORON S., «Formation of a Coalition-Proof Stable Cartel», *The Canadian Journal of Economics / Revue Canadienne d'Economique*, no. 31, 1998, pages 63-76.

VICKERS J., «Delegation and the Theory of the Firm», *Economic Journal*, no. 95, 1985, pages 138-147.

The Make-or-Buy Choice in a Mixed Oligopoly: A Theoretical Investigation

Roberto Cellini - **Luca Lambertini** *

University of Catania   University of Bologna
and
University of Amsterdam

We take a game theory approach to study the make-or-buy decisions of firms in a mixed duopoly. We assume that a managerial firm and a profit-oriented firm compete in a duopoly market for a final good, and they can choose whether making an intermediate input or buying it from a monopolistic upstream firm. We find that different equilibria may arise, depending on parameter constellations. In particular, if the technology used for the production of the intermediate input is too costly, then the internal organization of firms at equilibrium is mixed, creating a conflict with social preferences that would always privilege vertical integration to outsourcing. [JEL Classification: C72, L13, L22]

1. - Introduction

A wide debate is currently taking place concerning the convenience for firms of making or buying intermediate goods to be used as inputs in the production process. This issue is closely related to choice between vertical integration and dis-integration, or, equivalently, with the opportunity of outsourcing.

From a historical perspective, the evolution of capitalism is characterised by different phases, in each of which the tendencies to vertical integration or vertical dis-integration are more or less intense. Even if we confine our attention to the last decades, the economic development of industrialised countries over the period

* <cellini@unict.it>, Department of Economics and Quantitative Methods; <luca.lambertini@unibo.it>, Department of Economics.

113

of the so-called economic boom (the Fifties and Sixties) seemed to be characterised by high incentives towards vertical integration. On the opposite, the Eighties witnessed a strong tendency to dis-integration, often interpreted as a way to increase flexibility (see Tadelis, 2002, *inter alia*). What is happening today, in the years of (the third wave of) "globalisation" is not clear, and this is reflected by a large literature discussing the various aspects of this issue over the last twenty years.[1]

According to Grossman and Hart (1986), the failure of the internal incentive system, due to an incomplete assignment of property rights within the integrated firm, may provide an advantage for arm's length relationships. Additionally, the existence of a sufficiently competitive upstream market where firms may access intermediate inputs and raw materials at relatively low prices may lure more and more firms to choose outsourcing, with a remarkable bandwagon effect driving this process. If this effect is strong enough, then firm idiosyncratic levels of vertical integration within a given industry are unlikely to obtain at the equilibrium (see McLaren, 2000; Grossman and Helpman, 2002, 2005; Antras and Helpman, 2004; see also Yeats, 1998, for an empirical assessment on the significance of outsourcing and global production sharing).

On the other hand, it is by now part of the acquired wisdom that vertical integration can be considered as a remedy to the well known *hold-up* problem, with particular reference to situations where vertically related firms must rely on incomplete contracts to trade intermediate inputs whose quality (or performance) is unobservable and requires costly investments (Williamson, 1971; Grossman and Hart, 1986).

Several other factors may of course intervene to make the picture even more complicate, such as technological shocks, market integration, the co-existence of firms with different goals, and so on.

In this paper we examine one of these extensions, and propose a very simple theoretical model predicting that different outcomes

---

[1] For an exhaustive account of the earlier literature on vertical integration, see PERRY M.H. (1989).

114

can emerge when firms with different objective functions compete in an oligopoly market. In particular, we take into consideration a duopoly model in which a standard profit-oriented firm competes *à la* Cournot with a managerial firm, in the market for the final good. The production of the final good requires, on a one-to-one basis, an intermediate input which can be either made in house by the downstream firms or bought from a monopolistic upstream firm. We characterise the optimal choice of firms as to the make-or-buy alternative, and prove that the equilibrium outcome is sensitive to the relative size of the market for the final good and the fixed cost of production associated to the intermediate input. In particular, our analysis shows that if the fixed cost required by the production of the intermediate input is low enough, then making the input *in house* is a dominant strategy for both firms, while otherwise the profit-seeking unit prefers outsourcing, giving thus rise to an industry with a mixed industry structure where vertical integration and outsourcing do coexist at equilibrium. By contrast, vertical integration is always socially preferable to outsourcing in view of its beneficial effect on the equilibrium price of the final good and therefore on consumer surplus.

Note that in the present paper we confine ourselves to a partial equilibrium framework. Of course, a general equilibrium perspective could lead to different conclusions and policy prescriptions (see, *e.g.*, Feenstra and Hanson, 1996, on the relationship between outsourcing and wage inequality in the globalized world; Arora and Gambardella, 2006 and Bianchi et al., 2006 for recent analysis of the role of outsourcing in the "old" and "new" industrial policy).

The structure of the paper is as follows. Section 2 presents the layout of the model. Section 3 focuses on a comparative assessment of the alternative equilibria and a selection among them. Section 4 contains a few concluding comments.

2. - The Structure of the Model

We consider a situation in which two firms, 1 and 2, compete on the market of a final good characterised by the following inverse demand function:

(1)
$$P = a - Q, \quad a > 0$$

Firms compete under complete and symmetric information à la Cournot, simultaneously setting the amount of production, q_1 and q_2 respectively.

Firm 1 is assumed to be managerial; in particular, following Vickers (1985), we assume that the managers aim at maximising a weighted average of profit and production, while the owners are able to write the contract for managers in such a way that the managerial incentive is "optimally" set so as to maximise their firm's profits. Firm 2 is a standard profit-oriented firm. Hence, the objective function of the firms during the market subgame are, respectively:

(2)
$$V_1 = \pi_1 + tq_1 = (a - Q)q_1 - C_1 + tq_1, \quad t \geq 0$$

(3)
$$V_2 = \pi_2 = (a - Q)q_2 - C_2$$

where π_i (i=1,2) denotes profits (that is, the difference between revenues and operative costs C_i); variable t (in eq. (2)) measures the managerial incentive, which has to be appropriately chosen by the firm's owners.

The production of one unit of output q requires one unit of an intermediate input, that can be either (i) produced by the same firms, or (ii) bought in the upstream input market. Its production entails a fixed cost k and a marginal cost of production c>0, irrespective of whether it is produced by firm 1 and/or 2 internally, or outsourced. However, in the latter case, its unit price is w>0.

This means that production cost under the case in which firm(s) 1 and/or 2 decide to make it (make-option) is

(4)
$$C^m_i = cq_i + k, \quad c > 0, i = 1,2$$

while the cost function under the buy-option is

(5)
$$C^b_i = wq_i, \quad i = 1,2$$

If the intermediate good is produced by a different firm (called firm *U*, standing for *upstream*), we assume that such a firm enjoys a monopoly power in the upstream market and sets the unit price *w* in order to maximise its profits.[2]

The stage-by-stage sequence of decisions along the time line of the game is represented in Graph 1.

GRAPH 1

THE TIMING OF DECISIONS

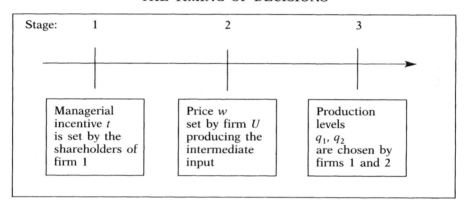

At stage 1, the owners of firm 1 determine the incentive coefficient *t*; this variable has an "institutional" flavour, so that it is natural to assume that it is fixed at the outset.

At stage 2, the monopolistic firm (possibly) producing the intermediate input sets the unit price of its product; the price is set optimally in order to maximise profits, and looking ahead at the demand expressed by one or both firms operating in the market for the final good.

At stage 3, the duopolistic downstream firms noncooperatively and simultaneously choose their respective output levels, in order to maximise their objective functions.

We evaluate the results for firms and consumers, in the four

---

[2] For a model where downstream firms face a competitive upstream market, see GARVEY G.T. - PITCHFORD R. (1995).

cases corresponding to the choice of making or buying the intermediate input by each downstream firm. This amounts to say that the decision on whether making or buying the input is taken at stage 0, and entails an irreversible commitment.

3. - Solving Subgames

3.1 *Both Firms Make the Intermediate Input*

We start by considering the case in which both firms decide to produce the intermediate input. This case is denoted by the *m* (make) or *mm* (make-make) appearing at the superscript of the relevant functions and variables. As usual, the game is solved by subgame perfection obtained through backward induction.

At the last stage of the game, firm 1 faces the problem:

(6)
$$\underset{q_1}{Max}: V_1^m = [a - (q_1 + q_2)]q_1 - cq_1 - k + tq_1$$

while firm 2 solves the following problem:

(7)
$$\underset{q_2}{Max}: V_2^m = [a - (q_1 + q_2)]q_2 - cq_2 - k$$

The first order conditions, $\partial V_1^m/\partial q_1 = 0$, $\partial V_2^m/\partial q_2 = 0$ give the reaction function system, whose intersection yields the Cournot-Nash equilibrium output levels:

(8)
$$\begin{cases} q_1^{mm} = \dfrac{1}{3}(a - c + 2t) \\ q_2^{mm} = \dfrac{1}{3}(a - c - t) \end{cases}$$

The above expressions depend on the reservation price, parameter a, the marginal cost c, and t, which is perceived as given at this stage of the game. Notice in particular that the delegation

118

extent, t, affects not only the level of production of the managerial firm, but also the production of his opponent, who finds it
optimal to reduce the production as a reaction to the output
expansion undertaken by firm 1, as it is usually observed in a
Cournot market game with substitute goods.

In this case, no decision has to be taken by the firm producing
the intermediate input, since it does not face any positive demand
for its product.

Substituting the values of q_1^{mm} and q_2^{mm} in the profit function
of firm 1 and simplifying, one may write the profit function of
firm 1, and then select the value of t maximising it. This procedure
yields the optimal extent of strategic delegation:

(9) $$t^{mm} = (a-c)/4$$

In turn, it is immediate to find the corresponding value for
individual production levels, profits, consumer surplus and social
welfare (defined as the sum of firms' profits and consumer surplus):

(10)
$$
\begin{cases}
q_1^{mm} = (a-c)/2 \\[4pt]
q_2^{mm} = (a-c)/4 \\[4pt]
\pi_1^{mm} = \dfrac{(a-c)^2}{8} - k \\[8pt]
\pi_2^{mm} = \dfrac{(a-c)^2}{16} - k \\[8pt]
CS^{mm} = \dfrac{9}{32}(a-c)^2 \\[8pt]
SW^{mm} = \dfrac{15}{32}(a-c)^2 - 2k
\end{cases}
$$

As expected, the firm whose owners delegate to a manager
the decision about production can gain a higher profit with respect to a standard profit-seeking (entrepreneurial) firm, thanks
to the expansion in the production level. This result is well known

119

from the pioneering work of Vickers (1985) and Fershtman and Judd (1987), *inter alia*.

Note also that a (simple) parametric condition must be imposed on k, in order to ensure positive profits for both firms, *i.e.*, $k<(a-c)^2/16$.

3.2 *Both Firms Buy the Intermediate Input*

If both firms commit themselves to buy the intermediate input, they face the following maximum problems:

$$(11) \qquad \underset{q_1}{Max} V_1^b = [a-(q_1+q_2)]q_1 - wq_1 + tq_1$$

$$(12) \qquad \underset{q_2}{Max} V_2^b = [a-(q_1+q_2)]q_2 - wq_2$$

From the first order conditions, which are omitted for the sake of brevity, we derive the Nash equilibrium at the market stage, as follows:

$$(13) \qquad \begin{cases} q_1^{bb} = \dfrac{1}{3}(a-w+2t) \\ q_2^{bb} = \dfrac{1}{3}(a-w-t) \end{cases}$$

Also in this case, the managerial coefficient affects the choice of both the managerial firm and his opponent, in opposite directions.

The expressions appearing in system *(13)* also provide the total amount of the intermediate input to be bought from the upstream firm, provided that the input requirement is supposed to be one unit of input per unit of output.

Hence, the firm producing the intermediate input (firm U) faces the following profit function:

$$(14) \qquad \pi_U^{bb} = (w-c)(q_1^{bb}+q_2^{bb}) - k$$

where w is the market price of the intermediate input, whose production entails in this case as well a fixed cost k and a marginal (constant) cost equal to c.

As firm U enjoys monopoly power, it can set the price of its output in order to maximise profits *(14)*; in particular, note that its profit function appears to be concave in w, once the firm, correctly anticipating the demand for its good deriving from the downstream firms, has plugged outputs *(13)* into *(14)*. The optimal pricing rule for the upstream monopolist is then summarised by the following condition:

$$(15) \qquad \frac{\partial \pi_0^{bb}}{\partial w} = 0 \Rightarrow w^{bb} = \frac{2(a+c)+t}{4}$$

By substituting *(15)* in *(13)* and then *(13)* in the profit function of firm 1, one obtains

$$(16) \qquad \pi_1^{bb} = (2a - 2c - 5t)(2a - 2c + 7t)/144$$

which is concave in t. The value of t providing the maximum profit is then

$$(17) \qquad t^{bb} = 2(a - c)/35$$

which measures – using the label suggested by Vickers (1985) – the optimal extent of the delegation of control to managers.

As a last step, we are now able to compute the price of the intermediate input set by the upstream monopolist producing the intermediate input, the level of production chosen by the duopolistic firms in the market for the final consumption good and the corresponding profits, consumer surplus and social welfare (defined as the sum of the profits of three firms, and the consumer surplus in the market for the final good):

(18)
$$\begin{cases} w^{bb} = (18a + 17c)/35 \\ q_1^{bb} = (a-c)/5 \\ q_2^{bb} = (a-c)/7 \\ \pi_1^{bb} = \dfrac{(a-c)^2}{35} \\ \pi_2^{bb} = \dfrac{(a-c)^2}{49} \\ CS^{bb} = \dfrac{72}{1225}(a-c)^2 \\ SW^{bb} = \dfrac{348}{1225}(a-c)^2 - k \end{cases}$$

A straightforward comparison between expressions *(10)* and *(18)* produces a number of interesting insights.

First of all, the levels of production of the final good are much lower in the case of a "buy" decision. Each firm shrinks its own production and consequently the aggregate production in the market of final good decreases of an amount equal to $Q^{bb} = (57/140)(a-c)$. Hence, the associated decrease in consumers' surplus amounts to $(8721/39200)(a-c)^2$. This means that consumers prefer a situation in which both firms decide to make the intermediate input, as compared to the situation in which both firms decide to buy it from the upstream monopolist. The economic intuition is as follows. In the buy-buy game, outsourcing entails *(i)* higher production costs for the final good, which bring about *(ii)* a decrease in aggregate output and clearly *(iii)* an increase in the equilibrium price. This chain of implications obviously implies that outsourcing ultimately hurts consumers.

Second, the variation in individual profits for the firms producing the final goods may take both signs, depending on the size of k; however, the difference between the profits of the two firms is smaller in the case of buy-buy as compared to the make-make situation.

Third, from a social perspective, $SW^{bb} - SW^{mm} = k - (7239/39200)(a-c)^2$ again may take both signs, depending on the relative size of k and $(a-c)^2$.

3.3 *The Managerial Firm Makes the Intermediate Input while the Profit-Seeking One Buys It*

In the mixed case in which the managerial firm decides to make the intermediate input internally while the standard neo-classical (profit-oriented) firm decides to buy it, the relevant objective functions are *(6)* and *(12)*, respectively. The usual procedure to compute the first order conditions, to obtain the reaction functions, and then to compute the Nash equilibrium output levels leads to following result:

(19)
$$\begin{cases} q_1^{mb} = \dfrac{1}{3}(a - 2c + 2t + w) \\[2mm] q_2^{mb} = \dfrac{1}{3}(a + c - t - 2w) \end{cases}$$

Also in this case, as one could expect from the outset, the extent of the managerial delegation positively affects the production level of the managerial firm, and negatively affects the production level of his opponent. More interestingly, the marginal production cost of the intermediate good, c, has a direct (and negative) effect on the production level of firm 1, and a (direct) positive effect on the production level of firm 2. Moreover, the market price level of the intermediate good, w, has a (direct) negative effect on the level of production of firm 2 and a (direct) positive effect on the production level of firm 1. However, one has to take into account that the production cost c clearly affects the price of the intermediate input set by the monopolistic upstream firm, so that the whole effects are not clear-cut *a priori*.

Note that q_2^{mb} in *(19)* also represents the demand function for the intermediate input faced by firm U, whose objective turns out to be

(20) $\quad \underset{w}{Max}\, \pi_U^{mb} = (w - c)(q_2^{mb}) - k = (w - c)(a + c - t - 2w)/3 - k$

The solution of firm U's maximum problem is

(21)
$$w^{mb} = (a + 3c - t)/4$$

Needless to say, the comparison between the levels of the input price provided by *(18)* and *(21)* is not a straightforward one, due to the fact that the upstream monopolist producing the intermediate input faces a different demand function in the case in the two alternative settings, with the inequality depending upon parameters a and c, as well as variable t. Of course, the effect of t on the input price is negative, since a higher extent of delegation entails a higher production for firm 1, and correspondingly a lower one for firm 2, which ultimately means that there will be a lower demand for the intermediate input provided by firm U.

The optimal value for t can be computed maximising the profits of firm 1. By substituting *(21)* into *(19)*, and then *(19)* into *(6)*, one finds that the profits of firm 1 in this case are

$$(22) \qquad \pi_1^{mb} = \frac{25(a-c)^2 + 10(a-c)t - 35t^2}{144} - k$$

from which it is immediate to find the optimal value of t, *i.e.*,

$$(23) \qquad t^{mb} = (a-c)/7$$

Then, substituting *(23)* back into all of the relevant variables and simplifying, one can fully characterise the equilibrium outcome of this setting:

$$(24) \quad \left\{ \begin{aligned} w^{mb} &= (3a+11c)/14 \\ q_1^{mb} &= (a-c)/2 \\ q_2^{mb} &= (a-c)/7 \\ \pi_1^{mb} &= \frac{5(a-c)^2}{28} - k \\ \pi_2^{mb} &= \frac{(a-c)^2}{49} \\ CS^{mb} &= \frac{81}{392}(a-c)^2 \\ SW^{mb} &= \frac{171}{392}(a-c)^2 - 2k \end{aligned} \right.$$

Interestingly enough, in this "mixed" situation, where firm 1 makes the intermediate input in house, while firm 2 buys it, firm 1 ends up producing the same amount of final good as in the case in which both firms make the input, and firm 2 produces the same amount of final good as in the case in which both firms buy the input. Thus, the aggregate production level of the final good lies between the cases in which both firms adopt the same decision whether to buy or make the intermediate input.

The viability condition in this setup consists in requiring that the equilibrium profits of the managerial firm be positive, *i.e.*, $\pi_1^{mb} > 0$. This is equivalent to imposing that $k < 5(a-c)^2/28$. This obviously suffices to ensure that $SW^{mb} > 0$ as well.

3.4 *The Managerial Firm Buys the Input while the Entrepreneurial One Makes It*

If firm 1 buys the intermediate input while his opponent decides to make it, firms' objective functions are defined as in *(11)* and *(7)*, respectively. The Nash equilibrium at the market stage is:

(25)
$$\begin{cases} q_1^{bm} = \dfrac{1}{3}(a+c+2t-2w) \\[2mm] q_2^{bm} = \dfrac{1}{3}(a-2c-t+w) \end{cases}$$

The qualitative properties of system *(25)*, as far as the influence of a, c, t and w on output levels is concerned, are largely the same as in the previous cases.

Considering that q_1^{bm} in *(25)* represents the demand function for the intermediate input, the goal of firm U now writes:

(26) $$\underset{w}{Max}\, \pi_U^{bm} = (w-c)(q_1^{bm}) - k = (w-c)(a+c+2t-2w)/3 - k$$

The solution is

(27) $$w^{bm} = (a+3c+2t)/4$$

In this case, in which the managerial firm buys the input, the higher the delegation extent t, the higher the price of the intermediate input. The intuitive explanation for this fact is that delegation makes the managerial firm richer as well as bigger than its rival; under full information, this feature is exploited by the upstream monopolist by driving the input price upwards.

Variable t can be computed taking into account profit of firm 1 once (27) is substituted in (25), and then in the profit function, which can be rewritten as:

$$(28) \quad \pi_1^{bm} = \frac{(a-c-4t)(a-c+2t)}{36} = -\frac{2}{9}t^2 - \frac{1}{18}(a-c) \cdot t + \frac{1}{36}(a-c)^2$$

The above expression takes its maximum in correspondence of $t = -(a-c)/8$, and is decreasing in t for all positive values of t. This means that the optimal extent of delegation is $t^{bm}=0$ (that is, we explicitly exclude the possibility of writing output-reducing delegation contracts). The economic interpretation is very simple, as the owners of firm 1 are aware that managers find it optimal to expand the output (and therefore also the demand for the intermediate input which has to be bought in the market). This leads to lower profits if the intermediate input is outsourced. Accordingly, shareholders find it optimal to set the output expansion incentive to zero, entailing that the managerial firm indeed mimics the behaviour of a pure profit-seeking enterprise.

Substituting $t=0$ back into all the relevant variables and simplifying, we obtain

$$(29) \quad \begin{cases} w^{bm} = (a+3c)/4 \\ q_1^{bm} = (a-c)/6 \\ q_2^{bm} = 5(a-c)/12 \\ \pi_1^{bm} = \frac{(a-c)^2}{36} \\ \pi_2^{bm} = \frac{25(a-c)^2}{144} - k \\ CS^{bm} = \frac{49}{288}(a-c)^2 \\ SW^{bm} = \frac{119}{288}(a-c)^2 - 2k \end{cases}$$

Here, the viability condition for the above equilibrium outcome to be admissible is $\pi_2^{mb}>0$, or equivalently $k<25(a-c)^2/144$. In this case, the profit of firm 2 is larger than her opponent's, for all $k<(7/48)(a-c)^2$. Note that this is necessarily the case, as the latter condition is milder than the viability condition.

Consumers surely prefer the opposite situation where firm 1 makes and firm 2 buys rather than the present one. This is motivated by the fact that the managerial firm is free to expand output when the intermediate input is made in house, and this factor has an obvious effect on aggregate output.

3.5 *Comparison*

Table 1 provides a detailed overview of the foregoing analysis, concerning equilibrium outputs, downstream firms' profits, consumer surplus and social welfare.

From the consumers' standpoint, the best situation is the case in which both firms decide to make the input, followed by the

TABLE 1

A SUMMARY OF EQUILIBRIUM OUTCOMES

	mm	*bb*	*mb*	*bm*
q_1	$(a-c)/2$	$(a-c)/5$	$(a-c)/2$	$(a-c)/6$
q_2	$(a-c)/4$	$(a-c)/7$	$(a-c)/7$	$5(a-c)/12$
π_1	$\dfrac{(a-c)^2}{8}-k$	$\dfrac{(a-c)^2}{35}$	$\dfrac{5(a-c)^2}{28}-k$	$\dfrac{(a-c)^2}{36}$
π_2	$\dfrac{(a-c)^2}{16}-k$	$\dfrac{(a-c)^2}{49}$	$\dfrac{(a-c)^2}{49}$	$\dfrac{25(a-c)^2}{144}-k$
CS	$\dfrac{9}{32}(a-c)^2$	$\dfrac{72}{1225}(a-c)^2$	$\dfrac{81}{392}(a-c)^2$	$\dfrac{49}{288}(a-c)^2$
SW	$\dfrac{15}{32}(a-c)^2-2k$	$\dfrac{348}{1225}(a-c)^2-k$	$\dfrac{171}{392}(a-c)^2-2k$	$\dfrac{119}{288}(a-c)^2-2k$

127

case in which only the managerial makes, followed in turn by the case where only the profit-oriented firm decides to make. The worst situation is the case where both firms decide to buy. This is motivated by the fact that outsourcing by the entire industry ultimately involves the highest market price for the final good. This is summarised by

LEMMA 1. $CS^{mm} > CS^{mb} > CS^{bm} > CS^{bb}$ always.

Now take the social perspective. A quick inspection of the equilibrium social welfare levels in the four alternative settings reveals:

PROPOSITION 2. For all $k < (a-c)^2/16$, $SW^{mm} > SW^{mb} > SW^{bm} > SW^{bb}$.

That is, provided the fundamental viability condition is met, then social preferences fully reflect the ranking of consumer surplus levels stated in Lemma 1.[3] Note that Proposition 2 implies a non-trivial result, *i.e.*, that the situation where one fixed cost is saved because of a generalised industry outsourcing decision, is not as appealing as it might look *ex ante*. That is, avoiding the duplication of the fixed component of the input cost is not a desirable achievement *per se*, since it involves the undesirable effect of inducing a price increase in the market for the final good. In other words, the make-make decision, even if entails fixed costs' duplication, turns out to be socially preferable to alternative situations where such a duplication does not occur, since it entails a larger level of final output and hence a higher consumer surplus.

There remains to investigate the strategic interplay between firms 1 and 2 when it comes to choose whether to make or buy the input. Table 2 illustrates the reduced form of the make-or-buy game, from the downstream firms' viewpoint.

Maintaining the hypothesis that the game is played once and firms cannot bear negative payoff on this market, *i.e.*, $k < (a-c)^2/16$, we see that M is always a strictly dominant strategy for the managerial firm (firm 1), while it is a strictly dominant strategy for the entrepreneurial firm (firm 2) as well if and only

---

[3] The condition whereby $SW^{bm} > SW^{bb}$ is $k < 0.284\,(a-c)^2$, which is surely met if $k < (a-c)^2/16$.

Table 2

THE MAKE-OR-BUY GAME BETWEEN DOWNSTREAM FIRMS

Firm 1 \ Firm 2	M		B	
M	$\dfrac{(a-c)^2}{8}-k$	$\dfrac{(a-c)^2}{16}-k$	$\dfrac{5(a-c)^2}{28}-k$	$\dfrac{(a-c)^2}{49}$
B	$\dfrac{(a-c)^2}{36}$	$\dfrac{25(a-c)^2}{144}-k$	$\dfrac{(a-c)^2}{35}$	$\dfrac{(a-c)^2}{49}$

if $k < 0.042\,(a-c)^2$. Outside this parameter range, up to $k < (a-c)^2/16$, firm 2 prefers to buy if firm 1 makes, while it prefers to make if firm 1 buys. Note that, in the latter case, the 2x2 matrix can be reduced by deleting the second row (due to the fact that M is dominant for firm 1); this allows us to conclude that, on what remains of the original matrix (the top row), B is dominant for firm 2, for all $k \in (0.042(a-c)^2, (a-c)^2/16)$. Accordingly, we can state:

PROPOSITION 3. For all $k < 0.042(a-c)^2$, (M,M) is the unique Nash equilibrium (in weakly dominant strategies). For all $k \in (0.042(a-c)^2, (a-c)^2/16$ (M,B) is the unique Nash equilibrium (attainable by iterated dominance).

In words, this amounts to say that for low levels of fixed cost of production the unique equilibrium entails that both firms choose to make the input in house. For higher levels of fixed costs, the equilibrium entails that the managerial firm produces the input in house while the profit-oriented firm resorts to outsourcing.

Propositions 2-3 immediately imply the following relevant corollary:

COROLLARY 4. For all $k < 0.042(a-c)^2$, there is no conflict between private and social incentives as to the make-or-buy decision. A conflict instead arises for all $k \in (0.042(a-c)^2, (a-c)^2/16)$ where (M,M) is socially preferred while (M,B) is privately selected.

A few comments are now in order. First, the option to buy the input (*i.e.*, outsourcing) becomes attractive for the profit-seeking unit if the fixed cost is high enough, while it is never so for the managerial firm. The intuitive reason appears to be that strategic delegation makes a firm richer than it would be otherwise (all else equal) and therefore more keen on resorting to vertical integration no matter what the cost is, while the entrepreneurial unit is weaker (or, equivalently, poorer) and therefore more sensitive to any given increase in the cost of the upstream technology. This gives rise to the possibility of observing a divergence between private and social incentives as to the make-or-buy choice, given that vertical integration of the entire industry is always socially preferable to any other scenario because of its desirable consequences on consumer surplus.

Second, a related issue is that the arising of such a conflict opens a discussion on industrial policy instruments, as the conflict itself could be avoided by subsidising the profit-seeking firm so as to induce it to internalise the production of the input notwithstanding its high fixed-cost component. The appropriate amount of resources to be redirected to the profit-seeking firm as a subsidy could be raised (either alternatively or jointly) from taxes levied on consumers and/or from the profits accruing to the managerial firm.

4. - Concluding Remarks

We have modelled a Cournot duopoly where a profit-seeking firm and a managerial one coexist and must choose whether to make or buy an intermediate input which contributes to the production of the final consumption good.

The situation has been represented by a simple three-stage game. At the first stage, each firm has to commit herself either to produce in house the input or to buy it on the market. Then, the other choices are taken: in turn, the owners of the managerial firm set the managerial incentive; the independent upstream firm producing the input sets its price; each duopolist sets her production level. The game has been solved by backward induction, yielding several interesting results (under the assumption that the parameter constellation allows both firms to obtain positive profits).

Taking a partial equilibrium perspective, we have shown that consumers always prefer the situation in which both firms choose in-house input production. This is also the best outcome from a social welfare perspective at the market level. Unfortunately, this is the equilibrium choice of firms only under a specific parameter configuration; if such a parameter condition is not met, a conflict arises between private and social preferences. However, the divergence could be eliminated, in principle, by designing an appropriate subsidy scheme for the profit-seeking firm.

Two remarks are appropriate to conclude, as a note of caution, and as insights for possible future research. First, we have maintained the hypothesis that the costs of in-house production of the input permit the duopolistic firms to obtain positive profits. Of course, the story could well go a different way, if a firm were *forced* to resort to outsourcing. Second, our analysis has been carried out in a partial equilibrium framework. Of course, different policy implications could emerge if a more general perspective was adopted.

BIBLIOGRAPHY

ANTRAS P. - HELPMAN E., «Global Sourcing», *Journal of Political Economy*, vol. 112, 2004, pages 552-580.

ARORA A. - GAMBARDELLA A., «Emerging Issues in the New Economy and Globalization», in BIANCHI P. - LABORY S. (eds.), *International Handbook on Industrial Policy*, Edward Elgar, Cheltenham, UK, 2006, pages 28-44.

BIANCHI P. - LABORY S. - PACI D. - PARRILLI M.D., «Small and Medium Sized Entreprise Policies in Europe, Latin America and Asia», in BIANCHI P. - LABORY S. (eds.), *International Handbook on Industrial Policy*, Edward Elgar, Cheltenham, UK, 2006, pages 380-401.

FEENSTRA R.C. - HANSON G.H., «Globalization, Outsourcing and Wage Inequality», *American Economic Review Papers and Proceedings*, vol. 86, 1996, pages 240-245.

FERSHTMAN C. - JUDD K., «Equilibrium Incentives in Oligopoly», *American Economic Review*, vol. 77, 1987, pages 927-940.

GARVEY G.T. - PITCHFORD R., «Input Market Competition and the Make-or-Buy Decision», *Journal of Economics and Management Strategy*, vol. 4, 1995, pages 491-508.

GROSSMAN G.M. - HELPMAN E., «Integration versus Outsourcing in Industry Equilibrium», *Quarterly Journal of Economics*, vol. 117, 2002, pages 85-120.

— — - — —, «Outsourcing in a Global Economy», *Review of Economic Studies*, vol. 72, no. 205, 2005, pages 135-159.

McLAREN J., «Globalization and Vertical Structure», *American Economic Review*, vol. 90, 2000, pages 1239-1254.

PERRY M.K., «Vertical Integration: Determinants and Effects», in SCHMALENSEE R. - WILLIG R.D. (eds), *Handbook of Industrial Organization*, vol. 1, Amsterdam, North-Holland, 1989, pages 183-255.

SAPPINGTON D., «On the Irrelevance of Input Prices for Make-or-Buy Decisions», *American Economic Review*, vol. 95, 2005, pages 1631-1638.

TADELIS S., «Complexity, Flexibility, and the Make-or-Buy Decision», *American Economic Review*, vol. 92, 2002, pages 433-437.

VICKERS J., «Delegation and the Theory of the firm», *Economic Journal*, vol. 95, Conference Papers, 1985, pages 138-147.

WILLIAMSON O., «The Vertical Integration of Production: Market Failure Considerations», *American Economic Review*, vol. 61, 1971, pages 112-123.

YEATS A., «Just How Big is Global Production Sharing», World Bank, Policy Research, *Working Paper*, no. 1871, 1998.

Entrepreneurs' Behaviour and Performance: An Empirical Analysis on Italian Firms

Filippo Oropallo - Stefania Rossetti*

ISTAT, Rome

This paper provides empirical evidence about differently performing Italian firms, using micro-data drawn from Istat structural business statistics. The analysis performed identifies four groups of firms that follow different strategies in terms of profits and productivity. The first is related to small dimensions, low quality of human capital, investment intensity. The second is mainly associated to sole proprietorships operating in family services. The third is positively associated to higher quality of human capital, investment and debt intensity. The fourth depicts large companies of northern regions involved in scale intensive sectors. Finally, multivariate techniques allow to quantify the impact of some variables on different profiles. [JEL Classification: L21, L25, L26]

1. - Introduction

The debate about the arguments of firms' objective function is undoubtedly one of the oldest and unresolved of industrial economics.[1] However, an even more puzzling and conceptually prior question concerns the very definition of entrepreneur and firm. Just to mention two of the most famous definitions we can remind Cantillon's view of the entrepreneur as someone who assumes the risk and may legitimately appropriate any profits and the Schumpeterian view, which depicts the entrepreneur as the

---

* <oropallo@istat.it>; <strosset@istat.it>.
[1] The main references are BAUMOL W. (1958); MARRIS R. (1963); PENROSE E. (1959); SOLOW R. (1971); WILLIAMSON O. (1966).

innovator who implements change within markets through the carrying out of new combinations.

We may actually argue that different visions about who an entrepreneur/firm is necessarily produce different visions about how an entrepreneur/firm behaves and consequently what their objectives are. In this case, the first definition suggests the idea of a profit seeking behaviour, while the second points to objectives such as productivity and growth.

In a broader sense, it seems that the definition of entrepreneur, of his behaviours and objectives are strictly interrelated and find proper attention in the study of entrepreneurship. Although, most literature on entrepreneurship is presently devoted to nascent economic activities and their entrepreneurial process,[2] we believe that the study of existing firms behaviour is equally useful for our comprehension of the productive system.

This paper, relying on a conceptual framework initially developed by Bruyat and Julien (2001) and revisited by Seymour (2006), provides empirical evidence about differently performing firms in Italy and their characteristics. The analysis performed helps to identify four groups of firms that follow different strategies in terms of profits and productivity. Multivariate techniques allow to investigate the underneath factors determining different performances.

The paper is organized as follows: next section presents the conceptual framework for the empirical analysis; the following one describes the data set used; the fourth section reports the results of the analysis; finally, in the last section some concluding remarks are provided.

2. - The Conceptual Framework: Different Objectives for Different Entrepreneurs

It is important to stress that entrepreneurship is an interesting issue not only for economists but also for sociologists, psy-

---

[2] That is all the functions, activities, and actions associated with start-ups and their actual realization (Bygrave W.D. - Hofer C.W., 1991).

chologists, behavioural and management scientists. However, independent disciplinary approaches are not capable to advance the knowledge and comprehension of entrepreneurial process which appears to be more and more complex (Fayolle, 2000). Actually the study of entrepreneurship seems a field where different sciences have mutually and beneficially integrated each other.

Many authors have also elaborated conceptual frameworks and models to describe and represent the entrepreneurial process. Most of them are based on the idea that the entrepreneurial behaviour is the result of an interactive process between environmental and individual factors (Fayolle, 2000).

To our ends, that is to describe profiles of differently performing entrepreneurs, an interesting framework is proposed by Bruyat and Julien (2001) and recently revisited by Seymour (2006). According to their notion entrepreneurship is the "dialogic"[3] between the "individual"[4] and new value creation, in which the environment can play an active role. Therefore, entrepreneurship is concerned first and foremost with a process of change and creation: creation of new value, but also, and at the same time, change and creation for the individual. According to Seymour (2006) the creation of new value can be interpreted as the creation of value for the others (employees, government, customers, ...), while the change for the individual is a process of value creation captured by the entrepreneur/firm himself. The combination of these two elements allows the authors to present a simple typology of entrepreneurial systems illustrating the heterogeneity of the field.

Combining the different "dimensions" of value creation, Graph 1 shows how different types of entrepreneurs may emerge. The top right box refers to those entrepreneurs that manage

---

[3] The dialogic principle defined by Morin E. (1989) means that two or more different elements are combined in a complex way in a single unit (their logics may be simultaneously complementary, concurrent and antagonistic), without their duality being lost in the combination.

[4] The notion of individual used by the authors takes account for the fact that sometimes, value creation originates from a team, not a single individual; therefore they use the following definition of the word "individual": «An organized, living body with its own existence that cannot be divided without being destroyed».

GRAPH 1

DIMENSIONS OF ENTREPRENEURIAL PERFORMANCE

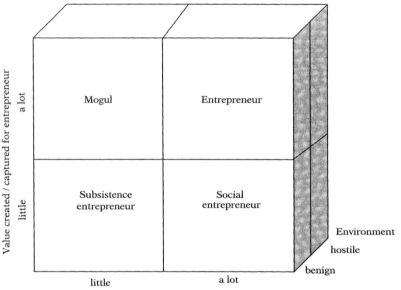

rapidly-growing firms producing a lot of value both for themselves and for others and may correspond to the idea of classic entrepreneurs (in Smith's sense). At the other hand (bottom left box) we find the firms who create little value and may be defined as "subsistence entrepreneurs". The top left box depicts the idea of "mogul", that is of the entrepreneur who produces value for himself but not for others. Last, the "social entrepreneurs" (bottom right box) produce more value for the community than for themselves. This should be the case of cooperatives or large companies, where proprietorship either is not defined, or is separated from management.

The empirical work presented in this paper attempts an assessment of this framework for Italy. The basic idea is that the action/processes represented by the axes of Graph 1 can be usefully represented by different performance variables of the firm: a profit maximising behaviour may approximate the vertical axis dimension; while growth and productivity may fit the horizontal axis.

3. - Data Description and Definition of Economic Indicators

The dataset used in this study is the result of an integration process of different statistical[5] and administrative sources. The Business Register (Asia) represents the population of reference and contains the structural characteristics of all Italian firms[6]. The Structural Business Statistics (Sbs)[7] consists of two surveys: all firms with at least 100 workers and a sample of smaller ones and find out accounting variables, some employment characteristics, investments and other features. In presence of lack of information, in particular for stock variables (assets and liabilities), balance sheets of limited liability companies have been used to reconstruct information. Moreover, thanks to the Foreign Trade statistics, it has been possible to link information about import-export activities.

The integration process[8] makes available a wide range of information for all Italian firms at a particular year of reference. This analysis is based on the last available Sbs data referred to 2004. Considering that a sample (63 thousands observations), representing all firms, has been analyzed, it hasn't been possible to utilize data of previous years, because the sample of small firms varies from one year to another. Panel data are only available for subsets of population (*i.e.* corporate firms, new firms).

In Table 1 the distribution of the population of Italian firms is illustrated. The sample represents 4.1 millions of firms (except agricultural, financial and non profit sector), employ 15.6 millions

---

[5] From ISTAT (National Statistical Institute of Italy) surveys.

[6] Except the agriculture and the non profit sector. See ISTAT (2006*a*).

[7] Sistema dei conti delle grandi imprese (Sci) and Rilevazione campionaria sulle piccole e medie imprese (Pmi). See ISTAT (2006*b*).

[8] See OROPALLO F. (2005).

TABLE 1

DISTRIBUTION OF FIRMS, WORKERS AND VALUE ADDED
(% values)

	Firms	Workers	Value added
Localization			
North-west	29.2	34.2	37.9
North-east	21.8	23.9	24.5
Centre	21.0	21.3	22.9
South and Islands	27.9	20.6	14.7
Size			
Micro (1-9 workers)	94.7	47.6	31.5
Small (10-49 workers)	4.7	21.7	23.3
Medium (49-249 workers)	0.5	12.6	16.9
Large (250 or more workers)	0.1	18.1	28.3
Legal form			
Sole proprietorship	45.2	21.1	10.7
Self employed, freelance	22.5	7.1	6.4
Partnership	19.1	18.2	12.8
Corporate company	12.2	47.8	66.0
Cooperative, other	1.0	5.7	4.1
Business sector			
Traditional manufacturing	8.0	14.4	14.8
Specialised supplier	1.4	4.6	6.4
Science based	0.8	2.0	3.5
Scale intensive	2.2	8.4	12.1
Energy, mining and quarrying	0.1	0.8	2.3
Construction	13.1	10.9	8.7
Trade	29.9	20.9	17.6
Hotels, restaurant, bar	6.1	6.4	3.3
Transport, telecommunication	3.8	7.3	10.4
Business services	23.7	16.4	15.0
Personal services	10.8	7.8	6.1

Source: Sbs surveys, Istat.

of workers (the average size in terms of workers is 3.8) and produce 567.6 billions of the national value added. They are almost all micro firms (95%), sole entrepreneurs and self employed (only 12% are companies) and one out of two is involved in trade and business services. If the value added is considered the contribution of northern regions, of medium and large firms, companies and industrial sector is stronger.

To measure economic behaviour at a firm level several indicators have been computed: the profitability indicator (equal to operating profits on sales); the apparent productivity indicator (equal to value added on workers); the share (on sales) of intermediate inputs, the debt intensity, as interest payments on sales; the years of activity; wages and salaries per employee.

Furthermore, to describe the competitive structure of markets a composite index has been used (see Calza *et* al., 2006). The index tries to embody barriers to competition that is the existence in each market, defined at a three digit Nace level, of non-competitive behaviours. According to this analysis there has been considered that capital requirements, advertising intensity and high concentration create obstacles to entry (apart from legal exclusions) (Bain, 1962), for that the synthetic index (mbi) combines three indicators: the concentration *ratio*, the share of advertising costs and the share of fixed assets.

4. - Empirical Evidence

4.1 *Typologies of Entrepreneurs and their Characteristics*

In order to identify groups of entrepreneurs who stick to different types of performance according to the scheme presented in Graph 1, we need to find variables that approximate the two types of entrepreneurs' action.

The constraints posed by the information available in our data set suggest us to use the return on sales (Ros) and the value added per employee (apparent labour productivity).

These variables may be considered as proxies respectively of the entrepreneur's ability to create value for himself and for others, as depicted in Graph 1[9].

---

[9] Cella P. *et* al. (2007) in a research on new entrepreneurs profiles study the dimensions of performance using a principal component analysis on a set of performance variables, which include growth rates of turnover, employment and labour productivity, vertical integration, levels of Ros and labour productivity.

GRAPH 2

DISTRIBUTION OF PRODUCTIVITY
(value added per worker)

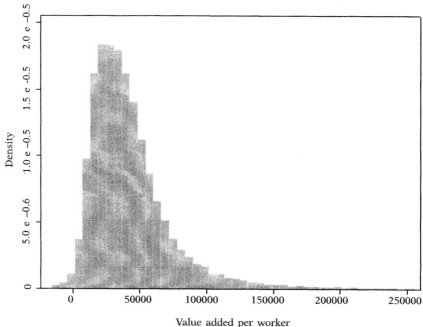

Value added per worker

Source: Sbs surveys, Istat.

The distribution of the value added per worker, the apparent labour productivity, presents a heavy positive asymmetry deriving from the fact that high levels of productivity are reached by only few firms.

Still in terms of shape, the distribution of profitability, that appears more symmetric, has a more acute peak around the mean (that is, a higher probability than a normally distributed variable of values near the mean) and fat tails (that is, a higher probability than a normally distributed variable of extreme values).

The scatter of these two variables in a bi-dimensional space, defined by the intersection of Ros and value added per worker at

GRAPH 3
DISTRIBUTION OF PROFITABILITY (ROS)

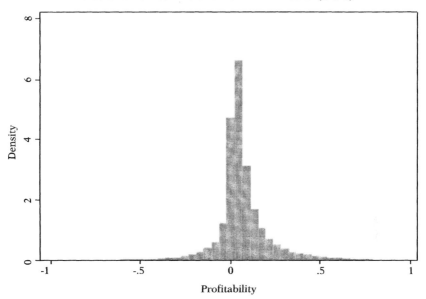

Source: Sbs surveys, Istat.

GRAPH 4
SCATTER PLOT OF PRODUCTIVITY AND PROFITABILITY

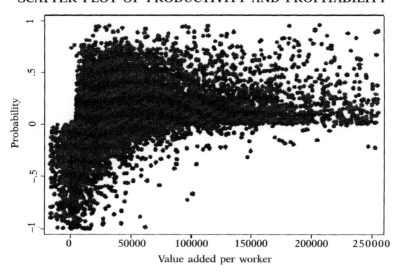

Source: Sbs surveys, Istat.

141

TABLE 2

PROFILES AND PERFORMANCE

Profile	% freq.	Return on sales[1]	Value added p.w.[2]	Workers	Interm. Inputs[3]	% debt intensity[4]	Years	% importing firms	% exporting firms	mbi
Subsistence	36.5	0.06	11	3.5	0.71	1.0	13	3.9	3.8	2.65
Mogul	26.0	0.61	14	1.2	0.31	0.6	12	0.2	0.5	2.73
Classic	19.8	0.65	47	1.6	0.26	1.1	13	0.6	1.4	2.78
Social	17.7	0.13	43	11.5	0.67	1.7	15	15.0	15.8	2.63
Total	100.0	0.33	25	4.0	0.50	1.0	13	4.2	4.6	2.66

Source: Sbs surveys, Istat.
[1] Operating profits on sales
[2] Value added per worker (apparent labour productivity) in thousand of euro
[3] Intermediate inputs on sales
[4] Interest payments on sales (in percentage values)

their respective mean values[10], takes into account both the asymmetry and the leptokurtic of the two indicators. The cross-distribution highlights the strong variability of behaviour that we try to pigeonhole in four categories.

TABLE 3

DISTRIBUTION OF PROFILES
(% values)

	Subsistence	Mogul	Classic	Social
Localization				
North-west	24.7	30.2	34.4	34.3
North-east	19.9	18.4	28.4	26.8
Centre	21.4	21.9	18.5	20.1
South and Islands	34.0	29.5	18.6	18.9
Size				
Micro (1-9 workers)	95.9	99.9	99.2	78.2
Small (10-49 workers)	3.8	0.1	0.8	19.0
Medium (49-249 workers)	0.3	0.0	0.0	2.5
Large (250 or more workers)	0.0	0.0	0.0	0.4
Legal form				
Sole proprietorship	57.0	55.5	22.0	26.7
Self employed, freelance	4.1	33.8	59.7	3.3
Partnership	24.9	9.9	14.5	27.2
Corporate company	12.2	0.7	3.7	41.0
Cooperative, other	1.8	0.0	0.1	1.8
Business sector				
Traditional manufacturing	9.8	6.9	3.4	11.7
Specialised supplier	1.2	0.7	1.1	3.8
Science based	0.6	1.1	0.6	1.0
Scale intensive	1.8	1.0	1.5	6.2
Energy, extraction	0.0	0.0	0.0	0.2
Construction	11.1	19.6	7.9	16.0
Trade	41.7	16.8	21.4	32.1
Hotels, restaurant, bar	12.3	2.6	1.2	4.1
Transport, telecommunication	2.8	4.7	3.1	6.2
Business services	10.9	31.6	43.2	15.2
Personal services	7.7	15.1	16.7	3.6

Source: Sbs surveys, Istat.

---

[10] Observations satisfying the double condition of a productivity level lower than +/- 20 per cent the mean level and a Ros level lower than +/- 0,3. The mean level have been deleted, since they may represent quite blurred cases (1,425 sample observations). Outlier values have been deleted as well.

The most numerous group is given by the "subsistence" entrepreneurs (36.5% of firms, 32% of workers and 12% of value added): their size is slightly lower than average, their profitability is about one fifth of the average and their labour productivity is less than half of the average level. They are overrepresented in the Southern regions, among the sole proprietorship or small partnerships and in the traditional tertiary and manufacturing sectors (trade, restaurants and hotels, textile and apparel, food, leather and shoes).

About one fourth of the firms may be classified as "moguls", but just 8% in terms of employment and 3% in terms of value added: their profitability levels are about twice the average, while the productivity is slightly more than the half of the average. Self-employed and free-lance are mostly represented in this group, whose average size is the lowest; they operate mainly in the construction sector and in business and personal services.

The group of classic entrepreneurs accounts for one fifth of the population of firms (8% in terms of employment and 11% of value added): productivity and profitability levels are doubled; their characteristics are quite similar to those of the moguls, although they are relatively more located in northern regions.

Finally, the group of "social" entrepreneurs (18%) employs more than half of the workforce (74% of value added): they include most of corporate firms, cooperatives and operate in scale economies sectors (public utilities, transport equipment, chemicals, etc.).

4.2 *Estimates of the Probability Models Type*

A further insight of the link between performance behaviours and other characteristics of the firm can be achieved using multivariate techniques. In the following we propose the estimate of a probability model for each type of firm. The probability of being one of the four typologies is assumed to be distributed according to a logistic cumulative distribution function. In this case the probability density function may be expressed as an exponential function, where arguments are the characteristics of the firm. If probabilities are divided by their reciprocal and after a logarithmic transformation, a linear probability model is estimated. In the transformed model, the logarithms of the odds *ratios* (*i.e.* the probability of a profile on the probability of the other profiles) depend on the characteristics of the firms.

The linear equation system is the following:

$$
(1) \begin{cases}
\log\left(\dfrac{p_i^{sub}}{1 - p_i^{sub}} \right) = \alpha + \sum_{l \in E} \beta_{l,i} E_{l,i} + \beta_{m,i} mbi_i + \sum_{j \in S} \beta_{j,i} X_{j,i} + \varepsilon_i \\[2ex]
\log\left(\dfrac{p_i^{mog}}{1 - p_i^{mog}} \right) = \alpha + \sum_{l \in E} \beta_{l,i} E_{l,i} + \beta_{m,i} mbi_i + \sum_{j \in S} \beta_{j,i} X_{j,i} + \varepsilon_i \\[2ex]
\log\left(\dfrac{p_i^{cl}}{1 - p_i^{cl}} \right) = \alpha + \sum_{l \in E} \beta_{l,i} E_{l,i} + \beta_{m,i} mbi_i + \sum_{j \in S} \beta_{j,i} X_{j,i} + \varepsilon_i \\[2ex]
\log\left(\dfrac{p_i^{soc}}{1 - p_i^{soc}} \right) = \alpha + \sum_{l \in E} \beta_{l,i} E_{l,i} + \beta_{m,i} mbi_i + \sum_{j \in S} \beta_{j,i} X_{j,i} + \varepsilon_i
\end{cases}
$$

where:
sub = subsistence firm, *mog* = mogul firm, *cl* = classic firm, *soc* = social firm
E_l = Set of economic indicators, X_j = Set of structural characteristics, *mbi* = market barrier index.

The independent variables included in the model take into account the economic behaviour of the firm (E_l = wage per employee, which is an indicator of the quality of human capital, investments, presence of exports or imports, debt *ratio*, service intensity inputs); the synthetic indicator of market barriers (*mbi*, see Par. 3) and some structural characteristics (X_j = size, sector, age, legal type, geographic area).

Estimated parameters of independent variables represent the partial derivative of the logarithmic odds *ratio* with respect to the independent variable. In the Table 4 the parameters in the exponential form ($e^{\beta i}$) are listed, in this case they measure the effect of a unitary change of an independent variable on the odds *ratio*. Levels higher (lower) than 1 means that an increase of the independent characteristic increases (reduces) the relative probability (odds *ratio*) of a profile.

TABLE 4
ESTIMATED PARAMETERS (IN EXP.) OF THE PROBABILITY MODEL

Firm's characteristics	Subsistence	Mogul	Classic	Social
Human capital	0.92	0.83	1.05	1.10
Service inputs	1.10	0.77	1.09	2.00
Debt intensity	0.97	1.10	1.69	0.83
Investment intensity	0.97	0.96	1.03	1.06
Import	0.68	0.20	0.33	1.68
Export	0.81	0.49	0.66	0.98
Market barriers	0.85	1.20	1.28	0.94
Years of business	0.78	0.93	1.37	1.40
Micro (except 1 worker)	2.38	0.41	0.63	1.43
Small	1.43	0.04	0.18	3.55
Medium	1.08	0.04	0.07	4.01
Large	1.61	(-)	0.07	2.67
North-east	1.04	0.79	1.25	0.93
Centre	1.37	1.12	0.69	0.80
South	1.92	0.89	0.55	0.76
Self employ-freelance	0.13	0.92	5.48	0.26
Partnerships	0.81	0.66	1.45	1.32
Corporate	0.74	0.08	0.44	2.32
Other	3.91	0.03	0.16	0.60
Textile products	0.43	3.93	4.33	0.42
Leather products	0.37	4.12	8.29	0.42
Wood products	0.39	3.09	3.72	0.73
Paper products	0.37	2.17	2.74	0.87
Coke, petroleum	0.04	(-)	5.45	3.16
Chemical products	0.43	0.59	1.62	1.19
Rubber products	0.35	1.37	3.74	(*)
Other non metallic	0.39	2.98	3.07	0.89
Metal products	0.20	2.95	9.83	(*)
Machinery	0.22	2.03	10.48	(*)
Electrical equipment	0.24	4.14	6.56	0.80
Transport equipment	0.44	1.86	4.73	0.83
Other manufactures	0.44	4.36	2.69	0.56
Energy sector	0.18	1.53	8.08	1.24
Construction	0.15	6.17	7.81	0.76
Trade	0.72	(*)	3.54	0.88
Hotel, Restaurants	1.29	0.89	1.44	0.47
Transport, telecomm.	0.16	3.74	7.51	1.04
Financial Services	0.08	4.28	16.02	0.42
Business Services	0.26	4.04	8.40	0.47
Education	0.61	4.84	4.40	0.20
Health	0.22	2.52	14.44	0.45
Other personal services	0.51	4.14	1.59	0.26
N. obs**	61,182	61,182	61,182	61,182
Pseudo R^2	42%	33%	34%	31%

(-) No observations.
(*) Parameter not significant.
(**) Sample observations represent 3.8 million of firms.

146

The analysis of the PseudoR^2 shows a good fit of the four models and the coefficients are statistically significant with few exceptions.

The results show that the quality of human capital has a negative impact on the probability of being either a subsistence firm or a mogul and a positive impact on the probability of being a classic or social firm. A similar behaviour is observed for other variables, namely the investment intensity, the years of activity and the export propensity. In general, these factors signal the border among high and low productivity firms. A high level of service inputs (that may be interpreted as an outsourcing indicators) has a strongly negative impact on the probability of being either a mogul or a classic type firm and is associated with low size of these firms; while the effect of intermediate inputs is sharply positive for subsistence firms. The debt intensity influence positively the probability of being either a subsistence or a classic firm. The market barrier index has a negative impact only on the probability of being a subsistence firm.

The geographical, sector and legal type dummies generally confirm the results described above. The most important effects are those of the south dummy which doubles the relative

TABLE 5

AVERAGE PROFILE PROBABILITIES

Mogul profile	0.71	*Classic profile*	0.65
Social and personal services	0.43	Self employed	0.53
Sole proprietorship	0.37	Health services	0.56
Less than 4 years	0.29	North	0.25
Centre-South	0.28		
Micro size	0.27		
Subsistence profile	0.83	*Social profile*	0.98
Restaurant/hotel sector	0.73	Scale intensity	0.89
Coop., other form	0.70	Medium-large	0.80
Less than 4 years	0.41	Corporate	0.55
South	0.46	More than 31 years	0.28
Micro size	0.38	North	0.20

probability of being a subsistence firm and halves that of being a classic firm. The corporate dummy strongly increases the relative probability of being a social type firm and decreases the others and in particular that of being a mogul. Finally, sector dummies show major influence on the classic profile.

An interesting application of the estimated probability may help to depict profiles computing their average probability. The characteristics of firms that maximize, for each type, the respective probability are in Table 5.

5. - Concluding Remarks

The main findings of the empirical analyses presented in the paper may be summarised as follows:

More than one third of Italian firms can be labelled as subsistence with levels of productivity and profitability lower than average. The elements that negatively influence the relative probability of this typology are the quality of human capital, investment intensity, international activities and the age of the firm. A typical profile of this group is given by (with a probability of 0.83) a restaurant or hotel, in cooperative form, with less than 4 years business activity, that operates in the south and with 1-9 employees.

The most relevant group, in terms of value added and employment, is given by the so called social firms. Their typical profile is an old large company of northern regions involved in scale intensity sectors. The investment intensity, the human capital quality and international activity positively affect the probability of this type.

Higher than average levels of profitability are associated to classic and mogul profiles, which represent respectively 20 and 26% of the firms, but just 11 and 3% of value added created. The probability of being a classic is positively affected by a higher quality of human capital, investment and debt intensity, market barriers, years of activity and by the share of service inputs. Partially opposite results come out for moguls and their typical profile seems to be a young micro firm, located in centre-south, sole proprietorship, operating in personal services.

Further studies could take into account the dynamics of firms behaviour, using panel data, characterizing more accurately the types of performances and the multiplicity of entrepreneurs' objectives.

BIBLIOGRAPHY

BAIN J.S., «Barriers to New Competition. Their Character and Consequences», *Manufacturing Industries*, Cambridge (MA), 1962.

BAUMOL W., «On the Theory of Oligopoly», *Economica*, vol. 25, 1958, pages 187-198.

BIGGERI L. - BINI M. - CALZA M.G. - OROPALLO F., «Factors Affecting the Success of New Entrepreneurs in Italy: A Multivariate Statistical Model Approach», *Cahier de la recherché*, Paris, ISC, 2007.

BIRCH D.L., *The Job Generation Process*, Department of Urban Studies and Planning, Cambridge (MA), MIT press, 1979.

BRUYAT C. - JULIEN P.A., «Defining the Field of Research in Entrepreneurship», *Journal of Business Venturing*, vol. 16, 2001, pages 165-180.

BYGRAVE W.D. - HOFER C.W., «Theorizing about Entrepreneurship», *Entrepreneurship Theory and Practice*, Winter, 1991, pages 13-22.

CALZA M.G. - CELLA P. - OROPALLO F. - ROSSETTI S. - VIVIANO C., *Data Integration for Entrepreneurship Indicators in Italy. Performance, Impact and Context Analysis*, presented at the Istat-Eurostat-Oecd, Workshop on Entrepreneurship Indicators, Rome, 2006.

CELLA P. - LAURETI T. - ROSSETTI S. - VIVIANO C., «New Successful Entrepreneurs in Italy: A Statistical Portrait», *Cahier de la recherché*, Paris, ISC, 2007.

FAYOLLE A., *Processus entrepreneurial et recherché en entrepreneuriat: les apporte d'un approche perceptuelle et empirique du domaine*, presented at the 5° Congrès International Francophone sur la PME, Lille, 2000.

ISTAT, «Struttura e dimensione delle imprese. Anno 2004», *Statistiche in breve*, Rome, 2006a.

— —, «Struttura e competitività del sistema delle imprese industriali e dei servizi. Anno 2004», *Statistiche in breve*, Rome, 2006b.

MARRIS R., «A Model of Managerial Enterprise», *Quarterly Journal of Economics*, vol. 77, 1963, pages 185-209.

MORIN E., «Diriger dans la complexité», conference on "Enterprise and Progress" Paris, March, in *Entreprises et Progrès*, June, 1989, pages 15-23.

OROPALLO F., «Enterprise Microsimulation Models and Data Challenges: Preliminary Results from the Diecofis Project», in FALORSI P.D. - RUSSO A. - PALLARA A. (eds.), *L'integrazione di dati di fonti diverse*, Milano, F. Angeli, 2005.

PENROSE E., *The Theory of the Growth of the Firm*, Oxford, Blackwell, 1959.

SEYMOUR R., «Measuring Entrepreneurial Activity», presented at the Istat-Eurostat-Oecd, Workshop on Entrepreneurship Indicators, Rome, 2006.

SOLOW R., «Some Implications of Alternative Criteria for the Firm», in MARRIS R. - WOOD A. (eds.), *The Corporate Economy*, London, Macmillan, 1971.

WILLIAMSON O., «Profit, Growth and Sales Maximisation», *Economica*, vol. 33, 1966, pages 1-16.

Firms' International Status and Heterogeneity in Performance: Evidence from Italy

Lorenzo Casaburi - **Valeria Gattai** - **G. Alfredo Minerva***

University of Bologna and Harvard University

University of Bologna and University 'L. Bocconi', Milan

University of Bologna

We revisit the evidence about firms' performance and their international status in a large sample of Italian enterprises. Three results stand out. First, firms engaging in foreign production of final goods, in addition to export activities, are more productive than firms that only export abroad. Second, firms engaging in final goods off-shoring are more productive than firms engaging in inputs off-shoring. Third, the productivity dynamics of exporters is not any better than non-exporters' one. Our results support that the better performance of globally engaged firms is chiefly due to the selection caused by the fixed costs associated to international operations. [JEL Classification: F10; F20; L10; L20; L60]

1. - Introduction

Recent years have seen remarkable changes in the nature of trade and FDI flows. Globalization has stretched national boundaries and broadened firms' perspective, making business an international issue. As a result, the international involvement of

---

* <casaburi@fas.harvard.edu>; <valeria.gattai@uni-bocconi.it>; <ga.minerva@uni-bo.it>.

The Authors thank Carlo Altomonte and Gianmarco Ottaviano for their guidance and Luca Lambertini for useful suggestions. This paper is prepared as a part of the Micro-Dyn research project, funded by the European Union under the VI Framework Programme. Financial support from the Italian Ministry for University and Research is also gratefully acknowledged. All remaining errors are attributable to the Authors.

151

firms has increased over time, and multinational enterprises have become key players of this globalized modern scenario.

Since international operations may be organized either "internally" — in wholly-owned subsidiaries — or "externally" — under arm's length contracts with independent local producers — the decision over the boundaries of multinational enterprises has received great attention by scholars worldwide.

While the make-or-buy choice of domestic producers was traditionally analysed by theorists of the firm, in the last few years, international economists made an attempt at extending those theories to the case of multinational enterprises. In doing so, they opened up the "black box", originally explored at the microeconomic level, while providing a simultaneous endogenization of the market environment, as in the international economics tradition.[1] In particular, it is possible to identify three paradigms — the Grossman-Hart-Moore treatment of hold-up and contractual incompleteness (Grossman - Hart, 1986; Hart - Moore, 1990), the Holmstrom-Milgrom view of the firm as an incentive system (Holmstrom - Milgrom, 1994) and the Aghion-Tirole conceptualisation of formal and real authority in organisations (Aghion - Tirole, 1997) — that have been embedded in industry and general equilibrium models, offering a complete characterisation of the interactions between ownership and location decisions of global companies. The boundaries of the Multinational Enterprise are thus shaped by a comparison between governance and transaction costs in the Grossman-Hart-Moore framework (see, among others: Grossman - Helpman 2002, 2003; Antras - Helpman, 2004; Antras, 2003; Feenstra - Hanson, 2003, 2004; Ottaviano - Turrini, 2007), by a trade-off between control and initiative in the Aghion-Tirole formalisation (Marin - Verdier, 2002, 2003), while in Holmstrom-Milgrom-based contributions outsourcing tends to be characterized by high powered incentives whereas integration emerges when workers earn a fixed wage and use firms' tools (Grossman - Helpman, 2004; Feenstra - Hanson, 2003, 2004).

Adding to intra-firm trade and vertical specialisation, one of

---

[1] For a survey see GATTAI V. (2006).

the most striking evidence of the last few years is the systematic relationship between firms' characteristics and their international involvement - including import, export and FDI activities. This evidence, in turns, has triggered academic research to better account for changes in trade and investment patterns, giving rise to theoretical and empirical refinements.

In theoretical terms, researchers have abandoned the representative firm's framework in favour of a new setting, due to Melitz (2003), in which firms are considered as heterogeneuos in terms of size and productivity. In Melitz's model, exposure to international trade leads more productive firms to export and less productive firms to exit the market, while further increases in an industry's exposure to trade induces an intra industry reallocation in favour of more productive firms. This approach has become the cornerstone of a growing literature that examines the role of heterogeneity in international trade and foreign direct investment, and its success derives from the fact that it provides rich predictions that can be easily confronted with the data.

In empirical terms, new challenges stem from the availability of extensive micro-level datasets, to test theoretical priors descending from heterogeneous firms' models.

Using firm-level data, researchers have documented that globally-engaged enterprises usually perform better than purely domestic ones. As a general result, exporters turn out to be a minority, and they tend to be more productive and larger (Tybout, 2003; Mayer - Ottaviano, 2007).

Looking at US manufacturing enterprises, Bernard - Jensen (1995, 1999) show that exporters are relatively rare and large in size. Indeed, even in tradable goods industries, the large majority of firms does not export and looks smaller than those engaged in international operations. Adding to this, exporters are more productive and capital-intensive, they pay higher wages, and employ more technology and skilled workers than non exporters. These results are completed and reinforced in Bernard *et* al. (2005) where the analysis is extended to all sectors of the US economy from 1993 to 2000, and also importers and foreign direct investors are included.

Eaton *et* al. (2004) examine French firm-level data and find that only 17% of total manufacturing firms were engaged in exporting activities in 1986, and export accounted only for 21% of their output, with lots of cross industry variations. Similar evidence is provided in Helpman *et* al. (2004) about US firms, Clerides *et* al. (1998) for Colombia, Mexico and Morocco, Aw *et* al. (2000) for Taiwan, Delgado *et* al. (2002) for Spain, Baldwin - Gu (2003) for Canada, Head - Ries (2003) for Japan, giving a sort of general consensus to the idea that international involvement and firms' performance are inextricably linked, irrespective of the nationality and the destination market.

This paper builds on the above mentioned empirical literature, and provides new evidence from a large sample of Italian firms. For the purpose of the present study, we have merged two waves of the Capitalia survey (1998-2000, and 2001-2003) retrieving firm level data for roughly 7,000 units. Given that this is one of the largest and more reliable sources of information about Italian enterprises, we are quite confident that the picture drawn here depicts quite well the relationship between performance and international status for Italy. Unfortunately we do not have data on importers, as in Bernard *et* al. (2005) and MacGarvie (2003), however we rank international status along several other categories such as export, vertical off-shoring, horizontal off-shoring and foreign affiliates. Hence, our study departs from the existing empirical literature in three regards: first, we introduce the off-shoring dimension, which was previously ignored; second, we adopt a finer classification of sectors, based on two-digits NACE instead of using macro industries as in Bernard et al. (2005); third, to go deeper into the topic, we analyze the productivity dynamics over time, and shed light on the difference between purely domestic and globally engaged companies in terms of TFP.

Three results are worth mentioning from this empirical exercise: first, firms that engage in the foreign production of final goods, in addition to export activities, are more productive than firms that only export abroad. Second, firms that engage in final goods off-shoring are more productive than firms that engage in inputs off-shoring. Third, in terms of the productivity dynamics over the period 1998-2003, exporters' performance in Italy was not any better than non-exporters' one.

The rest of the paper is organized as follows: section 2 provides a brief description of the dataset; section 3 contains the main definitions regarding firms' international status, and discuss whether exporters, off-shoring firms and foreign affiliates differ in their economic performance, through summary statistics and econometric regressions; section 4 is entirely dedicated to the productivity analysis, while section 5 concludes and sets future lines of research.

2. - Description of the Dataset

In this paper we use a panel of Italian manufacturing firms to explore the link between firms' performance and their international involvement. Our data are drawn from the Survey on Manufacturing Firms (*Indagine sulle Imprese Manifatturiere*) carried out by Capitalia, one of the largest Italian banks. We gather data from two subsequent waves, so that our time span goes from 1998 to 2003. The panel design is stratified and rotating, so that about half of the firms in the VIII wave (1998-2000) are dropped in the IX wave (2001-2003), with other new firms being added. The choice of firms to be dropped from the VIII wave, and of those to be added in the IX wave was casual, but still aimed at maintaining the stratified nature of the sample. Companies have been submitted a detailed questionnaire about their business, employment, R&D activity, internationalization and management. Additional balance sheet information has been derived from AIDA and *Centrale dei Bilanci*, two well-known and reliable sources of balance sheet data for Italy. The VIII wave of Capitalia contains detailed information on 4,680 firms. The IX wave of Capitalia gathered information on 4,289 firms, but we have balance sheet information for only 4,178 of them. In addition, we have only balance sheet information for other 5,511 firms over the period 2001-2003. The number of firms that is included both in the VIII wave and in the IX wave is 2,097.

Given the large number of observations, and the wide coverage in terms of geographic area, industry and size, we are quite confident that the data employed in this paper are highly representative of the Italian manufacturing sector.[2]

Our dataset provides information on firms that are purely domestic, exporters, and firms that engage in other forms of international activities (off-shoring, etc.). From our data, it is possible to sort exporters in two sub-categories, based on the destination market (EU, rest of the world), and to distinguish between off-shoring of final goods and off-shoring of inputs. Moreover, the dataset provides information about who controls the firm. It is then possible to know whether the control is exerted by a foreign resident, and in this case the firm can be classified as a foreign affiliate, as described below.

Before computing the descriptive statistics and performing the regressions, we identified a trimming procedure to get rid of some outliers (see Appendix A.1).[3]

3. - Main Features of Italian Exporters, off-Shoring Firms and Foreign Affiliates

In this section, we first define the different dimensions of Italian firms' international status. Then, we provide summary statistics and simple econometric regressions to discuss whether economic performance varies with international involvement.

3.1 Defining the International Status: Export, Vertical off-Shoring, Horizontal off-Shoring, Foreign Affiliates

Our definition of "exporters" is based on the Capitalia

---

[2] See BARBA NAVARETTI G. *et* AL. (2007) for a comparison, along several dimensions, of firms in the Capitalia dataset with the universe of Italian firms.

[3] Statistics for exporters and off-shoring firms with industry breakdown were computed out of a few hundreds of firms. Consequently, we chose to exclude from descriptive statistics observations flagged in the trimming procedure in order to avoid that statistics be affected by outliers.

questionnaire. Indeed, firms are accounted to be exporters in the period 1998-2000 if they answered "yes" to the D1.1 question in the VIII wave (Has the firm exported at least part of its output in 2000?) and they are accounted to be exporters in the period 2001-2003 if they answered "yes" to the D1.1.1 question in the IX wave (Has the firm exported at least part of its output in 2003?).[4] Unfortunately we do not have data on imports.

Off-shoring firms are identified in detail just in the IX wave. They are those that answered "yes" to the D3.1 question (At the present time, does the firm carry out at least part of its production activity in a foreign country?). We can also distinguish between final goods' and inputs' off-shoring (question D3.2.1). We call the first *horizontal off-shoring*, and the second *vertical off-shoring*, the distinction being based on the type of product that is off-shored.

Thanks to question D3.2.5, there exists another way of detecting whether off-shoring is horizontal or vertical in nature, the distinction being now based on the final destination of the output produced abroad. If a firm has off-shored, it is classified as engaging in horizontal off-shoring if at least 50% of the output is sold abroad or is sold to final consumers in Italy. In other terms, a firm is classified to perform horizontal off-shoring if less than 50% of the output produced abroad is imported in Italy to be re-processed. If a firm has off-shored, and more than 50% of the output produced abroad is imported in Italy to be re-processed, then we say that the firm is involved in vertical off-shoring.[5]

As it is shown by Table 1, while there exists a strong correlation among the two ways of computing horizontal and vertical off-shoring, the correspondence is not perfect. A potential advantage of detecting horizontal and vertical off-shoring through question D3.2.5 is that, since it relies on thresholds based on shares, we are able to classify all off-shoring firms as either horizontal or vertical. Employing question D3.2.1,

---

[4] See *APPENDIX* A.2 for details about questions in the IX Capitalia survey.
[5] This definition of horizontal and vertical off-shoring mirrors that in BENFRATELLO L. - RAZZOLINI T. (2007).

TABLE 1

CORRESPONDENCE BETWEEN THE TWO WAYS OF COMPUTING HORIZONTAL AND VERTICAL OFF-SHORING EMPLOYED IN THE PAPER
(Question D3.2.1 and Question D3.2.5)

	Type of output offsh. (Q. D3.2.1)			
	Final goods (Horizontal)	Inputs (Vertical)	Both of them	Total (row)
Mainly re-processed in Italy (Vertical)	8	64	18	90
Mainly other destinations (Horizontal)	120	37	61	218
Total (column)	128	101	79	308

Final destination of output offsh. (Q. D3.2.5)

we are left with 79 firms (those that produce both final goods and inputs abroad) that we do not know how to classify. However, as Table 1 shows, the great majority of firms doing off-shoring of both final goods and inputs is not involved in mainly reprocessing off-shored output in Italy. For this reason, for the rest of the paper, we classify firms that simultaneously do inputs' and final goods' off-shoring together with firms that only do final goods' off-shoring.

It is possible also to single out "foreign affiliates" through the A7 question in both waves. Following standard international definitions, we define as foreign affiliates foreign business enterprises in which there is foreign direct investment; that is, foreign business enterprises directly or indirectly owned or controlled by one foreign person to the extent of 10 percent or more of the voting securities.

3.2 *Relevance of Exporters, Vertical off-Shoring, Horizontal off-Shoring, Foreign Affiliates*

In this section, we show a few tables about the relevance of exporters, off-shoring enterprises and foreign affiliates in our database in 2003. Table 2 displays the share of total sales and employment of exporters, relative to all firms belonging to the same (NACE2) industry.

A very high share of firms in the sample are exporters (75%). This number is higher than the one for the US reported in Bernard *et* al. (2008), where exporters represent only 18% of the total population[6]. Notice also that exporters account for a very large share of sales and employment, without remarkable cross industry variation.

In Table 3 exporters are first ranked according to their absolute amount of exports, in order to identify the top 1%, 5%

---

[6] This suggests that exporting firms are over represented in the Capitalia dataset. A possible explanation stems from the fact that, in the Capitalia sample, larger firms are over represented. As we know, there is a positive correlation between size and exporting behavior (see section 1).

TABLE 2

SHARE OF EXPORTING FIRMS IN: TOTAL SALES, EMPLOYMENT, AND TOTAL NUMBER OF FIRMS, BY (NACE2) INDUSTRY

	NACE	Sales share	Employment share	Percentage of Firms
Food & beverages	15	69%	75%	66%
Textiles	17	90%	89%	81%
Clothing	18	92%	87%	84%
Leather	19	96%	87%	86%
Wood	20	67%	69%	65%
Paper products	21	66%	72%	68%
Publishing and printing	22	65%	60%	48%
Coke, refined petroleum and nuclear fuel	23	86%	37%	34%
Chemicals	24	61%	81%	78%
Plastics and rubber	25	97%	94%	83%
Non-metal minerals	26	80%	74%	50%
Metals	27	96%	92%	78%
Metal products	28	85%	78%	64%
Mechanical machineries	29	96%	95%	90%
Office equipments and PC	30	99%	91%	67%
Electric machinery	31	85%	87%	82%
TV and radio transmitters	32	85%	93%	70%
Medical, precision and optical instruments	33	94%	91%	83%
Motor vehicles	34	89%	92%	75%
Other transportation	35	97%	97%	79%
Furniture; Other Manufacturing	36	96%	93%	86%
Total manufacturing		84%	87%	75%

and 10%; then, the share of total sales is computed, by (NACE2) industry and exporting performance. We thus measure to what extent firms that perform well in the world markets do that also at home. First of all, there is considerable variability among industries: while in some sectors the "exceptional exporters" share of sales at home is high, in other sectors this is not true. Among the sectors in which firms that perform particularly well abroad

Table 3

SHARE OF TOTAL SALES BY TOP 1%, 5% AND 10% EXPORTERS,
BY (NACE2) INDUSTRY

	NACE	Share of total sales belonging to 1%	Share of total sales belonging to 5%	Share of total sales belonging to 10%
Food & beverages	15	0%	5%	9%
Textiles	17	2%	8%	13%
Clothing	18	0%	11%	15%
Leather	19	0%	22%	24%
Wood	20	0%	4%	4%
Paper products	21	0%	8%	12%
Publishing and printing	22	0%	5%	5%
Coke, refined petroleum and nuclear fuel	23	10%	10%	25%
Chemicals	24	4%	9%	11%
Plastics and rubber	25	14%	19%	19%
Non-metal minerals	26	0%	4%	23%
Metals	27	5%	17%	17%
Metal products	28	3%	6%	25%
Mechanical machineries	29	11%	19%	19%
Office equipments and PC	30	18%	18%	22%
Electric machinery	31	4%	11%	18%
TV and radio transmitters	32	4%	12%	16%
Medical, precision and optical instruments	33	10%	22%	25%
Motor vehicles	34	23%	25%	26%
Other transportation	35	6%	16%	17%
Furniture; Other Manufacturing	36	4%	10%	14%
Total manufacturing		2%	5%	20%

do that also at home, the three top sectors are Motor vehicles, Plastics and rubber, and Office equipments and PC.

Table 4 further describes the distribution of top exporters. Export activity is very much concentrated: for instance, the top 1% of exporters is responsible for 32% of total exports.

TABLE 4
DISTRIBUTION OF EXPORTERS

	Number	Total exports (millions Euro)	% of total exports
Top 1%	31	19,700	32%
Top 5%	153	36,100	59%
Top 10%	306	44,400	72%
Total	3,057	61,600	100%

A similar exercise is provided for off-shoring firms. Table 5 displays the share of total sales and employment of off-shoring firms, relative to all firms belonging to the same (NACE2) industry.

TABLE 5
SHARE OF OFF-SHORING FIRMS IN: TOTAL SALES, EMPLOYMENT AND TOTAL NUMBER OF FIRMS, BY (NACE2) INDUSTRY

	NACE	Sales share	Employment share	Percentage of Firms
Food & beverages	15	1.0%	0.8%	0.8%
Textiles	17	20%	18%	13%
Clothing	18	58%	50%	39%
Leather	19	22%	28%	19%
Wood	20	18%	17%	8%
Paper products	21	0%	0%	0%
Publishing and printing	22	1.5%	2%	1.4%
Coke, refined petroleum and nuclear fuel	23	11%	26%	4%
Chemicals	24	5%	5%	5%
Plastics and rubber	25	5%	8%	5%
Non-metal minerals	26	13%	12%	1.4%
Metals	27	2%	1.0%	1.6%
Metal products	28	7%	9%	4%
Mechanical machineries	29	17%	16%	7%
Office equipments and PC	30	66%	45%	14%
Electric machinery	31	10%	11%	9%
TV and radio transmitters	32	12%	12%	5%
Medical, precision and optical instruments	33	47%	53%	11%
Motor vehicles	34	10%	16%	11%
Other transportation	35	4%	5%	10%
Furniture; Other Manufacturing	36	30%	22%	7%
Total manufacturing		12%	14%	7%

For the whole manufacturing sector, the percentage of firms that is producing output off-shore is 7%, with a considerable cross-industry variation. The industry with more off-shoring firms is Clothing, followed by Leather products, and Office equipments and PC. Variability across industries is high also in terms of sales share and employment share. The industries that are more intensely involved in off-shoring, in terms of domestic sales and domestic employment, are: Office equipments and PC; Clothing; Medical, precision and optical instruments.

Table 6 distinguishes off-shoring of final goods and inputs, according to question D3.2.1.[7] Analyzing the relative sales and employment shares according to the type of good produced abroad, while in Office equipments and PC, and Medical, precision and optical instruments, the horizontal off-shoring strategy is predominant, in the Clothing sector a considerable fraction of output and employment is generated by firms engaged in vertical off-shoring. In terms of number of firms, the majority of off-shoring firms in the Leather industry is engaged in vertical off-shoring.

Summing up, the evidence from the Capitalia dataset strengthens the claim that some traditional industries (such as Clothing and Leather) are strongly involved in off-shoring (particularly of the vertical type). This mode of international operations is also important for some categories of high-tech industries, such as Office equipments and PC, and Medical, precision, and optical instruments.

Unfortunately, due to data constraint, we cannot rank off-shoring firms in absolute terms as we did for exporters, nor we can give their distribution.

Table 7 displays the shares in terms of total sales, employment, and overall number by foreign affiliates in the sample, relative to all firms belonging to the same (NACE2)

---

[7] For each variable of interest (sales, employment, number of firms) the sum of the two columns in Table 6 for final goods off-shoring and inputs off-shoring could be different from the total reported in Table 5 due to the rounding of decimals, or to the fact that some firms reported to be off-shoring, but they did not specify the nature of the products off-shored.

TABLE 6

SHARE OF TOTAL SALES, EMPLOYMENT AND NUMBER OF OFF-SHORING FIRMS, BY (NACE2) INDUSTRY AND TYPE OF OFF-SHORED ACTIVITY

	NACE	Final goods			Inputs		
		Sales share	Employment share	Percentage of Firms	Sales share	Employment share	Percentage of Firms
Food & beverages	15	0.7%	0.4%	0.5%	0.3%	0.5%	0.3%
Textiles	17	12%	10%	8%	7%	7%	5%
Clothing	18	35%	34%	30%	23%	16%	9%
Leather	19	15%	16%	8%	7%	11%	10%
Wood	20	14%	11%	2%	4%	6%	6%
Paper products	21	0%	0%	0%	0%	0%	0%
Publishing and printing	22	0%	0%	0%	1.4%	2%	1.4%
Coke, refined petroleum and nuclear fuel	23	0%	0%	0%	11%	26%	4%
Chemicals	24	5%	5%	5%	0%	0%	0%
Plastics and rubber	25	4%	5%	3%	0.8%	2%	1.1%
Non-metal minerals	26	13%	12%	1.4%	0%	0%	0%
Metals	27	2%	1.0%	1.6%	0%	0%	0%
Metal products	28	5%	7%	3%	1.6%	2%	1.3%
Mechanical machineries	29	11%	9%	5%	3%	5%	2%
Office equipments and PC	30	66%	45%	14%	0%	0%	0%
Electric machinery	31	5%	6%	5%	5%	5%	4%
TV and radio transmitters	32	12%	12%	5%	0%	0%	0%
Medical, precision and optical instruments	33	35%	45%	7%	13%	8%	4%
Motor vehicles	34	5%	6%	7%	6%	10%	4%
Other transportation	35	2%	3%	7%	1.3%	1.4%	3%
Furniture; Other Manufacturing	36	26%	18%	4%	4%	4%	2%
Total manufacturing		8%	9%	5%	3%	4%	2%

TABLE 7

SHARE OF TOTAL SALES, EMPLOYMENT AND NUMBER OF FOREIGN AFFILIATES FIRMS, BY (NACE2) INDUSTRY

	NACE	Total no. of foreign affiliates	Sales share	Employment share	Percentage of foreign affiliates	Percentage among exporters	Percentage among non-exporters
Food & beverages	15	12	8%	9%	2%	3%	2%
Textiles	17	16	13%	11%	5%	6%	0%
Clothing	18	9	21%	17%	6%	6%	9%
Leather	19	4	3%	3%	2%	3%	0%
Wood	20	2	4%	4%	2%	3%	0%
Paper products	21	5	16%	17%	4%	7%	0%
Publishing and printing	22	10	23%	25%	9%	10%	9%
Coke, refined petroleum and nuclear fuel	23	2	2%	19%	7%	10%	5%
Chemicals	24	36	21%	27%	15%	17%	7%
Plastics and rubber	25	13	31%	25%	6%	7%	0%
Non-metal minerals	26	19	6%	10%	7%	12%	3%
Metals	27	18	26%	28%	11%	13%	3%
Metal products	28	29	16%	17%	5%	8%	1%
Mechanical machineries	29	74	24%	20%	12%	12%	9%
Office equipments and PC	30	1	73%	53%	8%	13%	0%
Electric machinery	31	20	28%	28%	12%	12%	9%
TV and radio transmitters	32	13	55%	55%	16%	21%	4%
Medical, precision and optical instruments	33	14	22%	17%	17%	15%	25%
Motor vehicles	34	10	11%	19%	14%	17%	5%
Other transportation	35	3	16%	16%	7%	9%	0%
Furniture; Other Manufacturing	36	14	3%	4%	5%	6%	2%
Total manufacturing		324	18%	19%	8%	9%	4%

industry for the year 2003. It also displays the relevance of foreign affiliates among exporters and non-exporters. Coherently with what one would expect, foreign affiliates are more represented among exporters than among non-exporters.

In Table 8 foreign affiliates are first ranked according to their absolute amount of sales, in order to identify the top 1%, 5% and 10%; then, the share of total sales is computed, by sales' performance, for the total of foreign affiliates.[8] The concentration in terms of sales for top foreign affiliates is smaller than in the case of top exporters.

TABLE 8

DISTRIBUTION OF FOREIGN AFFILIATES

	Number	Total sales (millions Euro)	% of total sales
Top 1%	3	3,450	11%
Top 5%	16	10,810	36%
Top 10%	32	15,390	51%
Total	324	30,070	100%

3.3 *Comparing Firm's Performance Based on their International Status*

In this section, we discuss whether international status is correlated with economic performance, to see if exporters, off-shoring firms and foreign affiliates are different from non exporting, non off-shoring, and domestically-owned enterprises.

First of all, as in Bernard - Jensen (1999), selected characteristics of firm i — such as sales, employment, capital per worker, value added per worker and average wage — are regressed

---

[8] We do not show the breakdown by industry for top 1%, 5%, and 10% foreign affiliates in terms of total sales, since the total number of foreign affiliates by industry is small. We only provide the breakdown of top firms for the whole manufacturing sector.

against an export dummy and industry fixed effects (j is the industry subscript), according to the following specification:

$$\ln X_i = \alpha + \beta*Export_i + \gamma*Industry_j + u_i$$

Actually, we run four separate regressions. In the first, we do not distinguish about the final destination of the export flows. In the remaining ones, we do distinguish among different destinations, employing the information provided by those firms that answered to question D1.2. In the second regression we consider an export dummy for firms that made some exports towards one of the 26 European Union partners of Italy. Then, in the third regression, the export dummy takes value one for those firms that made some exports to countries in the world other than those belonging to the EU. Obviously, if the firm makes shipments to both destinations, the export dummy takes value one in both regressions. In the last regression, we concentrate just on firms that were exporting towards both destination areas (EU and non-EU countries). Table 9 reports the estimates. Coefficients and p-values (in parenthesis) are displayed.

TABLE 9

EXPORTER'S PREMIA IN THE CAPITALIA DATASET

	All exporting plants	Destination		
		EU	Not EU	Both EU and non-EU
Log Sales	0.871 (0.000)***	0.567 (0.000)***	0.361 (0.000)***	0.452 (0.000)***
Log Employment	0.663 (0.000)***	0.458 (0.000)***	0.339 (0.000)***	0.409 (0.000)***
Log Capital per worker	0.231 (0.000)***	0.254 (0.003)**	0.007 (0.879)	0.062 (0.125)
Log VA per worker	0.262 (0.000)***	0.226 (0.088)*	-0.036 (0.576)	0.153 (0.802)
Log Average wage	0.068 (0.000)***	0.075 (0.045)**	0.430 (0.020)**	0.055 (0.002)**

The evidence indicates that exporters have a better performance than non-exporters along several dimensions. One would also expect that firms that are able to reach a larger number of foreign markets, or markets located at a greater distance, be better performing than other exporters. The emerging differences in performance according to destination areas do not support this view. Coefficients' estimates for firms that are involved in exporting both to the EU and to the rest of the world are not larger than for the rest of firms.

As a second step, the same firms' characteristics are regressed against an off-shoring dummy and industry fixed effects, according to the following specification:

$$\ln X_i = \alpha + \beta * Off\text{-}shoring_i + \gamma * Industry_j + u_i$$

Table 10 reports the estimates. Coefficients and p-values (in parenthesis) are displayed.

Firms that off-shore appear to be larger, more capital intensive, and pay higher wages than the rest of firms in the panel. One may wonder at this point whether these features of off-shoring firms are always true, irrespective of the product being

TABLE 10

OFF-SHORER'S PREMIA IN THE CAPITALIA DATASET

	All types of off-shoring	Types	
		Final products	Inputs
Log Sales	1.076	1.114	0.589
	(0.000)***	(0.000)***	(0.000)***
Log Employment	0.800	0.770	0.675
	(0.000)***	(0.000)***	(0.000)***
Log Capital per worker	0.350	0.421	0.050
	(0.000)***	(0.000)***	(0.649)
Log VA per worker	0.105	0.144	0.020
	(0. 279)	(0.223)	(0.898)
Log Average wage	0.050	0.088	-0.022
	(0.027)**	(0.002)***	(0.544)

off-shored. Analyzing firms that off-shore the production of final products (question D3.2.1), all the performance indicators, with the exception of value-added, are still positive and statistically different from zero. On the contrary, the firms that are off-shoring inputs appear to be just larger than the rest of firms in the panel, with the point estimates of the coefficients on sales and employment being smaller than in the case of final goods' off-shorers. Vertical off-shoring firms look bigger than other firms in the panel, but not as big as the horizontal off-shoring ones. Hence, vertical disintegration, and the off-shoring of inputs production, is associated, to some extent, to a less brilliant performance with respect to horizontal off-shoring.[9] Overall, also off-shoring firms turn out to be different from other firms in the sample.

As a third step, sales, employment, capital per worker, value added per worker and average wage are regressed against the foreign affiliate dummy and industry fixed effects, according to the following specification:

$$\ln X_i = \alpha + \beta * Foreign\_Aff_i + \gamma * Industry_j + u_i$$

Table 11 reports the estimates. Coefficients and *p*-values (in parenthesis) are displayed.

TABLE 11

FOREIGN AFFILIATE'S PREMIA IN THE CAPITALIA DATASET

	Foreign affiliates
Log Sales	1.143
	(0.000)***
Log Employment	1.045
	(0.000)***
Log Capital per worker	0.264
	(0.000)***
Log VA per worker	0.374
	(0.000)***
Log Average wage	0.158
	(0.000)***

---

[9] We further analyze this issue below, in Section 4, which is entirely dedicated to productivity analysis.

The performance indicators are all highly and positively correlated with the status of being a foreign affiliate firm: they are also different.

The evidence we have presented so far neatly shows that Italian firms involved in international operations (both actively, as exporters and off-shorers, and passively, as foreign affiliates) are different from other firms. All the performance indicators we considered are statistically larger in the case of firms characterized by some form of international status. As already pointed out in the literature (see, for example, Mayer - Ottaviano, 2007) the causality could run in both ways. One explanation is that only better performing firms can raise the funds necessary to overcome the fixed costs associated to international operations (in the case of exports and off-shoring) or can attract foreign investors (in the case of foreign affiliates). The other explanation is that firms being involved in international operations improve, through a learning process, their efficiency thanks to international exposure, widening the gap in terms of performance with the non-internationalized enterprises. In the section that follows we try to shed some light on this important issue, focusing on one specific performance measure: productivity.

4. - Total Factor Productivity and International Status

4.1 *Methodology*

In this section we focus on firms' productivity as our performance index. Our goal is two-fold. First, we want to check whether firms can be ranked in productivity terms according to their international status. Second, we want to test whether, in the Capitalia panel, internationalized firms experienced a faster growth in productivity with respect to other firms in the panel over the period 1998-2003.

We estimate a separate Cobb-Douglas production function for each of 14 different categories. These categories result from the aggregation of the 20 two-digit NACE sectors on the basis of technological similarities (see Table 12).

Table 12

SECTORAL DISAGGREGATION EMPLOYED FOR
THE TFP ESTIMATION

NACE		number of firms	Category
15	Food and beverage	625	1
17 18	Textiles Clothing	721	2
19	Leather	271	3
20	Wood	166	4
21 22	Paper products Printing and publishing	331	5
24	Chemicals	296	6
25	Rubber and plastics	319	7
26	Non-metal minerals	359	8
27 28	Metals Metal products	1,024	9
29	Non-electric machinery	816	10
30 31 32 33	Office equipment and computers Electric machinery Electronic material Medical apparels and instruments	499	11
34 35	Vehicles Other transportation	167	12
36.1	Furniture and musical instruments	295	13
Other 36	Other manufacturing	112	14
Total		6,001	

The production function for a generic category j can be written as follows (all variables are in logarithm):

(1) $\ln Y_{ijt} = \alpha_i + \beta_1 W_{ijt} + \beta_2 B_{ijt} + \beta_3 K_{ijt} + \omega_{it} + \varepsilon_{ijt}$

where Y_{ijt} is value added by firm i in category j in year t, deflated by the Producer Price Index for the appropriate two-digit NACE industry to the year 2000; K_{ijt} are fixed assets, deflated by the simple average of the deflators for all NACE sectors, as in Smarzynska Javorcik (2004); W_{ijt} is the number of white collars employed; B_{ijt} is the number of blue collars employed; ω_{it} is the productivity component. The statistical properties of the productivity residual change according to the estimator employed. Productivity is assumed to be time-invariant ($\omega_{it}=\omega_i$ for every year t) in the case of fixed effects estimation, while it is allowed to be time-variant in the case of the semi-parametric approach proposed by Levinsohn - Petrin (2003). We follow both procedures to derive the productivity residual.[10]

After the estimation of productivity at the firm level through fixed effects and the semi-parametric approach, we are set to disentangle whether firms differently involved in international operations can be sorted according to their productivity.

We first replicate Benfratello - Razzolini (2007), BR hereafter, based on the definition of horizontal and vertical off-shoring based on Q. D3.2.5 (see section 3):[11]

— *Purely domestic firms.* They do not export nor they are engaged in any off-shoring of production.

— *Purely exporting firms; exporters doing vertical off-shoring.* This category encompasses those firms who engage in exports only, and those firms doing exports and engaging in the off-shoring of output that is then mainly reprocessed in Italy.

— *Exporting firms doing horizontal off-shoring.* This category encompasses those firms that export and simultaneously engage in off-shoring of goods that are not mainly reprocessed in Italy.

---

[10] Notice that, as mentioned above, the trimming procedure is performed before the fixed effects and Levinsohn-Petrin estimators are run: trimming serves the purpose to flag single observations that are subsequently excluded from the estimation of the production function.

[11] Our approach in the estimation of the production function is different from BENFRATELLO L.- RAZZOLINI T. (2007) under several respects. Here we mention just the following two main reasons. First, they use just the IX wave while our dataset results from the merge of the VIII and IX wave. We esteem that the production function estimation is improved in this manner, since *(i)* for roughly a half of firms surveyed in the VIII and the IX wave the production function is estimated over a 6-year time period, instead than a 3-year period, and *(ii)* after merging the VIII and IX wave the total number of different firms used in the TFP estimation is roughly doubled. Second, they consider a production function where no distinction is made between skilled and unskilled workers, because they use total labor cost from balance sheet as the labor input. In the production function *(1)* we considered two separate labor inputs: the total number of skilled workers, and the total number of unskilled workers employed each year by the firm. This follows standard practices in the estimation of the production function, and allows us to control for the skill composition of the workforce, thus cleaning the TFP residual from this component.

The evidence presented in Graph 1 (fixed effects) and Graph 2 (Levinsohn and Petrin) is consistent with the theory (Helpman *et al.*, 2003), and with other previous works for Italy or other countries. Purely domestic firms are less productive than firms engaging in export. In turn, firms that engage in export and horizontal off-shoring are more productive than firms that engage only in export or in export and vertical off-shoring. We then checked whether the aforementioned pattern is robust to a different way of computing the horizontal and vertical off-shoring status (this time following Q. D3.2.1). Results, reported for the Levinsohn and Petrin methodology only, are virtually unaffected, as shown in Graph 3.

GRAPH 1

PLOT OF THE CUMULATIVE DISTRIBUTION FUNCTION OF TFP:
PURELY DOMESTIC, EXPORTERS, HORIZONTAL OFF-SHORERS
(FIXED EFFECTS METHOD; BR CLASSIFICATION)

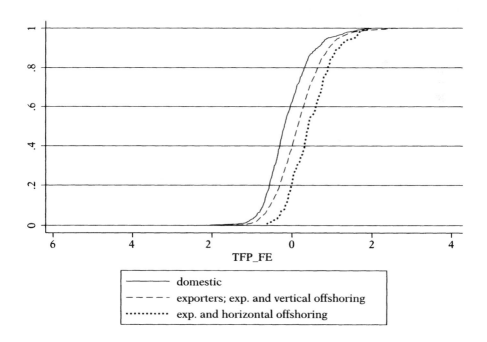

GRAPH 2
PLOT OF THE CUMULATIVE DISTRIBUTION FUNCTION OF TFP:
PURELY DOMESTIC, EXPORTERS, HORIZONTAL OFF-SHORERS
(LEVINSOHN-PETRIN METHOD; BR CLASSIFICATION)

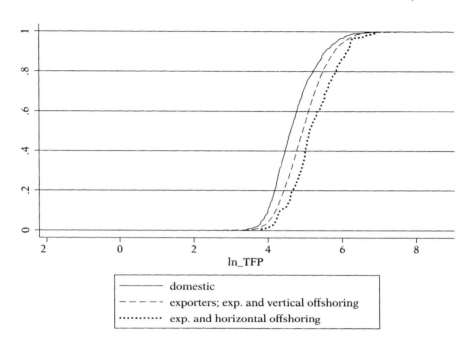

Then, we turn to another issue. Estimates from Table 10 show that, on average, off-shoring firms are better performers than non-off-shoring firms. However, final goods off-shoring and inputs off-shoring firms behave differently, with the former performing on average better than the latter. Abstracting from the role of exports, we then try to sort firms in productivity terms according to the type of good that is off-shored. Saying it in another way, we study whether firms that off-shore final goods are more productive than firms that off-shore inputs, and whether these two groups of firms are different from purely domestic enterprises.

For this purpose, we consider three different modes of internationalization:

Graph 3
PLOT OF THE CUMULATIVE DISTRIBUTION FUNCTION OF TFP: PURELY DOMESTIC, EXPORTERS, HORIZONTAL OFF-SHORERS (LEVINSOHN-PETRIN METHOD; CLASSIFICATION BASED ON QUESTION D3.2.1)

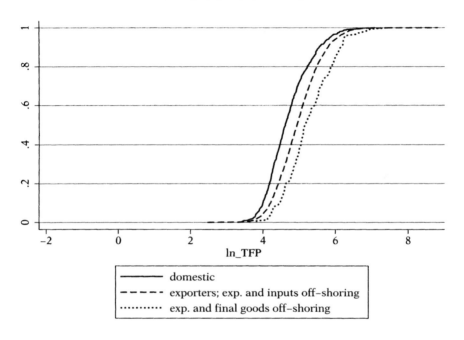

— *Purely domestic firms*. They do not export nor they are engaged in any off-shoring of production.

— *Vertical off-shoring firms*. Firms that off-shore only inputs of production.

— *Horizontal off-shoring firms*. Firms that off-shore only final goods, or both final goods and inputs.

For each mode, we compute the cumulative distribution functions, and plot them simultaneously in Graph 4 (fixed effects) and Graph 5 (Levinsohn and Petrin). Firms that off-shore inputs turn out to be more productive than purely domestic firms. They also turn out to be less productive than firms doing horizontal off-shoring, consistently with results from Table 10. What is

175

GRAPH 4

PLOT OF THE CUMULATIVE DISTRIBUTION FUNCTION OF TFP:
PURELY DOMESTIC, INPUTS OFF-SHORING, FINAL GOODS
OFF-SHORING (FIXED EFFECTS METHOD; CLASSIFICATION
BASED ON QUESTION D3.2.1)

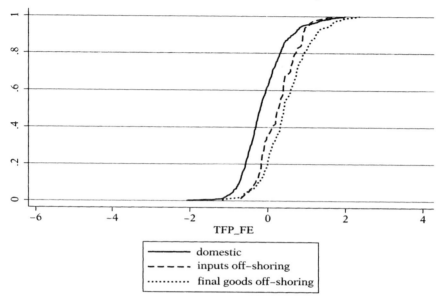

driving such a sorting in productivity terms? The evidence is consistent with the existence of fixed costs that are the lowest for domestic firms, intermediate for vertical off-shoring, and the highest for horizontal off-shoring. The existence of fixed costs may explain why only more productive firms are able to off-shore production, and why, among off-shoring firms, only the most productive of them are able to off-shore final products. For example, firms doing horizontal off-shoring may need marketing activities for their products (advertising, the search of local representatives abroad, etc.), which constitute an extra cost that is not incurred by firms engaged in vertical off-shoring.

Generalizing our findings, to the extent that different degrees of involvement in international operations are associated to different fixed costs (e.g., pure exporting *vs.* exporting and horizontal off-shoring; vertical off-shoring *vs.* horizontal off-

Graph 5

PLOT OF THE CUMULATIVE DISTRIBUTION FUNCTION OF TFP:
PURELY DOMESTIC, INPUTS OFF-SHORING, FINAL GOODS
OFF-SHORING (LEVINSOHN-PETRIN METHOD; CLASSIFICATION
BASED ON QUESTION D3.2.1)

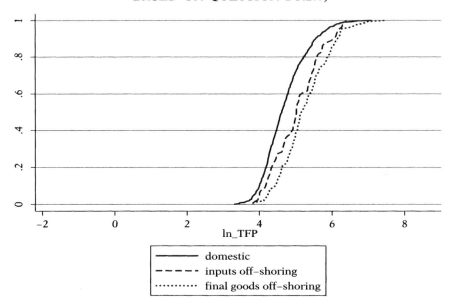

shoring), firms are expected to be naturally sorted by the modes
of international operations according to their productivity level,
and this is precisely what we observe in the data.

4.2 *Evolution Over Time of Productivity Indices: Exporters, non-Exporters, Foreign Affiliates*

The evolution over time of aggregate productivity indices can
be used to assess whether Italian firms also behave differently in
dynamic terms according to their international status. This issue
is important since it helps us to understand the direction of
causality: from performance to international status (as we were
discussing above), or from international status to performance, or
both of them. If firms involved in international operations are

177

found to be better performing than non-internationalized firms also in dynamics terms, we can conclude that a sort of learning process is set in motion, by which firms exposed to international operations perform increasingly better than the others.

Productivity indices aggregate for each sector the production function's residuals computed according to the Levinsohn and Petrin methodology. There are several ways to build these indices. We follow Levinsohn - Petrin (1999) and Petrin - Levinsohn (2006). For each sector (one of the 14 categories identified before) and each year, we aggregate individual TFP through a weighted average, where the weights are given by each firm's value-added share with respect to total value added in that year of the category it belongs to. These indices are then normalized with respect to 1998 (the base year). The results are presented in Table 13 (all firms), Table 14 (non-exporters), Table 15 (exporters).[12]

Since there are a few hundreds of foreign affiliates in the sample, for this class we computed only the aggregate evolution of productivity for the whole manufacturing sector, normalized to the 1998 aggregate productivity level. The evolution of the index over the 1998-2003 period turns out to be: 1; 0.995; 1.034; 1.033; 1.000; 0.984.

It is interesting to note that, for the whole manufacturing sector, exporters' growth in aggregate productivity was not faster than non-exporters'. The exporters' advantage in terms of a higher level of productivity, which constitutes a well-documented empirical regularity, also in the present paper, does not seem to entail any difference in terms of the dynamics of productivity over the 6-year's period we analyzed. Similarly, the productivity dynamics of foreign affiliates in the sample cannot be ranked as being faster than that of non-exporters.

Generalizing our findings, to the extent that different degrees of involvement in international operations are not associated to a better productivity dynamics, Italian firms do not appear to be learning or improving their performance due to international

---

[12] As mentioned elsewhere, questions about off-shoring are present just in the IX wave, so this prevented us from building productivity indices also for this internationalization mode.

Table 13

EVOLUTION OVER TIME OF THE PRODUCTIVITY INDEX: ALL FIRMS

NACE		Category	1998	1999	2000	2001	2002	2003
15	Food and beverage	1	1	0.998	0.999	0.988	0.967	0.971
17 18	Textiles Clothing	2	1	1.003	1.004	1.022	1.020	1.010
19	Leather	3	1	0.999	1.004	1.039	1.042	1.027
20	Wood	4	1	1.017	1.035	1.052	1.065	1.064
21 22	Paper products Printing and publishing	5	1	1.014	1.048	1.089	1.080	1.089
24	Chemicals	6	1	1.013	1.012	1.042	1.033	1.079
25	Rubber and plastics	7	1	1.011	1.013	1.083	1.084	1.079
26	Non-metal minerals	8	1	1.016	1.034	1.065	1.080	1.071
27 28	Metals Metal products	9	1	1.008	1.008	1.047	1.038	1.029
29	Non-electric machinery	10	1	0.992	0.982	1.050	1.048	1.026
30 31 32 33	Office equipment and computers Electric machinery Electronic material Medical apparels and instruments	11	1	1.009	1.061	1.024	1.011	0.996
34 35	Vehicles Other transportation	12	1	1.002	1.028	1.027	1.012	1.002
36.1	Furniture and musical instruments	13	1	1.005	1.027	1.133	1.114	1.075
Other 36	Other manufacturing	14	1	0.975	0.971	1.021	0.959	0.974
	Average manufacturing		1	1.005	1.030	1.038	1.027	1.025

179

TABLE 14

EVOLUTION OVER TIME OF THE PRODUCTIVITY INDEX: NON-EXPORTERS

NACE		Category	1998	1999	2000	2001	2002	2003
15	Food and beverage	1	1	1.008	1.024	1.032	1.030	1.039
17 18	Textiles Clothing	2	1	1.008	1.014	1.075	1.065	1.060
19	Leather	3	1	1.001	1.031.	1.083	1.061	1.039
20	Wood	4	1	1.028	1.038	1.029	1.045	1.080
21 22	Paper products Printing and publishing	5	1	1.018	1.035	1.080	1.088	1.085
24	Chemicals	6	1	1.002	0.920	1.029	1.025	1.018
25	Rubber and plastics	7	1	1.004	1.011	1.090	1.064	1.068
26	Non-metal minerals	8	1	1.022	1.049	0.995	0.975	0.995
27 28	Metals Metal products	9	1	1.009	1.008	1.046	1.037	1.039
29	Non-electric machinery	10	1	0.985	0.948	1.067	1.068	1.055
30 31 32 33	Office equipment and computers Electric machinery Electronic material Medical apparels and instruments	11	1	1.005	1.066	1.158	1.167	1.141
34 35	Vehicles Other transportation	12	1	1.012	1.066	0.849	0.833	0.825
36.1	Furniture and musical instruments	13	1	1.012	1.021	1.075	1.067	1.062
Other 36	Other manufacturing	14	1	0.948	0.924	0.939	0.940	0.942
	Average manufacturing		1	1.008	1.022	1.080	1.079	1.088

TABLE 15

EVOLUTION OVER TIME OF THE PRODUCTIVITY INDEX: EXPORTERS

NACE		Category	1998	1999	2000	2001	2002	2003
15	Food and beverage	1	1	0.996	0.990	0.967	0.929	0.928
17 18	Textiles Clothing	2	1	1.002	1.003	1.016	1.016	1.005
19	Leather	3	1	0.999	1.002	1.039	1.043	1.028
20	Wood	4	1	1.016	1.033	1.023	1.035	1.032
21 22	Paper products Printing and publishing	5	1	1.009	1.045	1.056	1.055	1.057
24	Chemicals	6	1	1.014	1.021	1.033	1.022	1.088
25	Rubber and plastics	7	1	1.010	1.012	1.077	1.079	1.075
26	Non-metal minerals	8	1	1.013	1.022	1.085	1.106	1.095
27 28	Metals Metal products	9	1	1.008	1.007	1.039	1.030	1.020
29	Non-electric machinery	10	1	0.992	0.982	1.047	1.045	1.023
30 31 32 33	Office equipment and computers Electric machinery Electronic material Medical apparels and instruments	11	1	1.009	1.057	1.020	1.008	0.994
34 35	Vehicles Other transportation	12	1	1.001	1.012	1.052	1.045	1.033
36.1	Furniture and musical instruments	13	1	1.004	1.027	1.126	1.108	1.068
Other 36	Other manufacturing	14	1	0.976	0.972	1.028	0.961	0.977
	Average manufacturing		1	1.005	1.030	1.028	1.016	1.013

exposure. Going back to the causality issue, we find weak support to the view that the better performance of international firms is caused by the involvement in international operations.

5. - Concluding Remarks

In this paper we analyzed the evidence concerning the link between firms' performance indicators — such as sales, employment, capital per worker, value-added per worker, average wage, productivity — and their involvement in international operations. More precisely, we distinguished between purely domestic firms, exporters, vertical off-shorers, horizontal off-shorers and foreign affiliates to capture different degrees of international exposure. Our results suggest that, as elsewhere documented in the literature (see, for a survey, Tybout, 2003) there exist wide differences in performance according to firms' international involvement. Moreover, in dynamics terms, we found scanty evidence on a differential performance of firms according to the export status. Our results support the view that the better performance (in static terms) of globally engaged firms is chiefly due to the selection caused by fixed costs associated to international operations.

It should be noted that our classification is by no means exhaustive of the different modes of internationalization, since it is possible to conceive other ways of classifying them. For instance, Barba Navaretti *et* al. (2007) note that exporters are not all alike, and further divide them in two sub-categories: those who export less than 40% of total sales, and those who export more than 40% of total sales.

This paper can be regarded as a first step in the direction of exploring the link between economic performance and international involvement of Italian enterprises, in that it provides new empirical evidence on the topic. Given the promising results achieved here, we believe that it is worth carrying out future research on this topic, trying to understand with greater accuracy the specific factors behind heterogeneity in performance.

APPENDIX

A.1. Trimming Procedure

Our trimming procedure consists in flagging observations with an extreme growth rate for any of the following variables: value added, capital, number of white collars, number of blue collars. We do not drop observations with extreme values in the growth rate of intermediates' consumption. In particular, we consider a growth rate as an extreme one if it belongs to the upper (99.5%) and bottom (0.05%) tails of the corresponding distribution across the firms in the panel, for a given couple of years. For example, observations for the years 2001 and 2002 are flagged if the growth rate in value added between 2001 and 2002 belongs to the bottom 0.5% of the distribution, or if it belongs to the upper 99.5% of the distribution.

A.2. Questions about Control, Export, and off-Shoring in the IX Capitalia survey

A7. *Firm's Control*

State, in a descending order in terms of voting securities owned, the characteristics of persons that own and/or directly control the business enterprise.

	Persons (keep anonymous)	* Type of person (see note)	Share of voting securities held by the person	Does the person exert a direct control on the firm?	Does the person has voting deals with others?
A7.1.	Person a	1 2 3 4 5	____ %	1. Yes 2. No	1. Yes 2. No
A7.2.	Person b	1 2 3 4 5	____ %	1. Yes 2. No	1. Yes 2. No
A7.3.	Person c	1 2 3 4 5	____ %	1. Yes 2. No	1. Yes 2. No
A7.4.	Others		____ %		
	Total		100 %		

*Indicate as follows:
1) Person non resident in Italy; 2) Physical person resident in Italy; 3) Italian business enterprise operating in manufacturing; 4) Italian business enterprise operating in services; 5) Italian banks and other Italian financial institutions.

D1. *Export*

D1.1.1 Has the firm exported at least part of its output in 2003? (Yes; No)

D1.2 Final geographic destination of exports, in percentage terms:

D1.2.1.	EU-15 countries	_____ %
D1.2.2.	Countries that joined EU in 2004	_____ %
D1.2.3.	Russia, Turkey and other European countries	_____ %
D1.2.4.	Africa	_____ %
D1.2.5.	Asia (apart from China)	_____ %
D1.2.6.	China	_____ %
D1.2.7.	United States, Canada and Mexico	_____ %
D1.2.8.	Central and South America	_____ %
D1.2.9.	Australia and Oceania	_____ %
	Total	100%

D3. *Off-Shoring*

D3.1. At the present time, does the firm carry out at least part of its production activity in a foreign country? (Yes; No)

D3.2. In which countries did you off-shore production? (Romania; Hungary; Croatia; Poland; Morocco; Tunisia; China; Others (specify)............)

D3.2.1 The firm off-shores production of:
Final goods (Yes; No)
Inputs or Components (Yes; No)
Both of them (Yes; No)

...

D3.2.5. Final destination of the production made abroad, in percentage terms

D3.2.5.1. Sold in the country where the productive unit is located: (%)

184

D3.2.5.2. Imported in Italy to re-enter the production process: (%)

D3.2.5.3. Imported to be sold on the Italian market: (%)

D3.2.5.4. Imported to be re-exported to third countries: (%)

D3.2.5.5. Sold directly to third countries: (%)

Total: 100 %

BIBLIOGRAPHY

AGHION P. - TIROLE J., «Formal and Real Authority in Organizations», *Journal of Political Economy*, vol. 105, 1997, pages 1-29.

ANTRAS P., «Firms, Contracts, and Trade Structure», *Quarterly Journal of Economics*, vol. 118, 2003, pages 1375-1418.

ANTRAS P. - HELPMAN E., «Global Sourcing», *Journal of Political Economy*, vol. 112, 2004, pages 552-580.

AW B.Y. - CHUNG S. - ROBERTS M.J., «Productivity and turnover in the export market: micro-level evidence from the Republic of Korea and Taiwan (China)», *World Bank Economic Review*, vol. 14, 2000, pages 65-90.

BALDWIN R.E. - GU W., «Export Market Participation and Productivity Performance in Canadian Manufacturing», *Canadian Journal of Economics*, vol. 36, 2003, pages 634-657.

BARBA NAVARETTI G. - BUGAMELLI M. - FAINI R. - SCHIVARDI F. - TUCCI A., *Le imprese e la specializzazione produttiva dell'Italia. Dal macrodeclino alla microcrescita?*, report presented at the conference «I vantaggi dell'Italia», Roma, Fondazione Rodolfo Debenedetti, 22 marzo 2007.

BENFRATELLO L. - RAZZOLINI T., *Firms' Productivity and Internationalization Choices: Evidence from a Large Sample of Italian Firms*, Valencia, 34th EARIE Conference, 6-9 September 2007.

BERNARD A.B. - JENSEN J.B., *Exporters, Job and Wages in US Manufacturing, 1976-1987*, Washington DC, Brookings Papers on Economic Activity, Microeconomics, 1995.

— — - — —, «Exceptional Exporter Performance: Cause, Effect or Both?», *Journal of International Economics*, vol. 47, 1999, pages 1-25.

BERNARD A.B. - JENSEN J.B. - SCHOTT P.K., «Importers, Exporters and Multinationals: A Portrait of Firms in the US that Trade Goods», *NBER, Working Paper*, no. 11404, 2005.

CLERIDES S.K. - LACH S. - TYBOUT R., «Is Learning by Exporting Important? Microdynamic Evidence from Colombia, Mexico and Morocco», *Quarterly Journal of Economics*, vol. 113, 1998, pages 903-947.

DELGADO M.A. - FARINAS J.C. - RUANO S., «Firm Productivity and Export Markets: A non Parametric Approach», *Journal of International Economics*, vol. 57, 2002, pages 397-422.

EATON J. - KORTUM S. - KRAMARZ F., «Dissecting Trade: Firms, Industries and Export Destination», *American Economic Review*, vol. 93, 2004, pages 150-154.

FEENSTRA R.C. - HANSON G.H., *Ownership and Control in Outsourcing to China: Estimating the Property-Rights Theory of the Firm*, University of California, Mimeo, 2003.

— — - — —, «Ownership and Control in Outsourcing to China: Estimating the Property-Rights Theory of the Firm», *NBER, Working Paper*, no. 10198, 2004.

GATTAI V., «From the Theory of the Firm to FDI and Internalization: A Survey», *Il Giornale degli Economisti e Annali di Economia*, vol. 65, 2006, pages 225-262.

GROSSMAN S.J. - HART O.D., «The Costs and Benefits of Ownership: a Theory of Vertical and Lateral Integration», *Journal of Political Economy*, vol. 94, 1986, pages 691-719.

GROSSMAN G.M. - HELPMAN E., «Integration *vs* Outsourcing in Industry Equilibrium», *Quarterly Journal of Economics*, vol. 117, 2002, pages 85-120.

GROSSMAN G.M. - HELPMAN E., «Outsourcing *vs* FDI in Industry Equilibrium», *Journal of the European Economic Association*, vol. 1, 2003, pages 317-327.

— — - — —, «Managerial Incentives and the International Organization of Production», *Journal of International Economics*, vol. 63, 2004, pages 237-262.

HART O.D. - MOORE J., «Property rights and the Nature of the Firm», *Journal of Political Economy*, vol. 98, 1990, pages 1119-1158.

HELPMAN H. - MELITZ M.J. - YEAPLE S.R., «Export versus FDI with Heterogeneous Firms», *American Economic Review*, vol. 94, 2004, pages 300-316.

HOLMSTROM B. - MILGROM P., «The Firm as an Incentive System», *American Economic Review*, vol. 84, 1994, pages 972-991.

LEVINSOHN J. - PETRIN A., «When Industries become More Productive, do Firms? Investigating Productivity Dynamics», *NBER, Working Paper*, no. 6893, 1999.

— — - — —, «Estimating Production Functions Using Inputs to Control for Unobservables», *Review of Economic Studies*, vol. 70, 2003, pages 317-341.

MACGARVIE M., *Do Firms Learn from International Trade? Evidence from Patent Citations and Micro Data*, Boston University School of Management, Mimeo, 2003.

MARIN D. - VERDIER T., «Power Inside the Firm and the Market: A General Equilibrium Approach», *CEPR, Discussion Paper*, no. 3526, 2002.

— — - — —, «Globalization and the Empowerment of Talent», *CEPR, Discussion Paper*, no. 4129, 2003.

MAYER T. - OTTAVIANO G.I.P., *The Happy Few: The Internationalisation of European Firms*, Bruegel, Blueprint Series, no. 3, 2007.

MELITZ M.J., «The Impact of Trade on Intra-industry Reallocations and Aggregate Industry Productivity», *Econometrica*, vol. 71, 2003, pages 1661-1694.

OTTAVIANO G.I.P. - TURRINI A., «Distance and FDI when Contracts are Incomplete», *Journal of the European Economic Association*, vol. 5, 2007, pages 796-822.

PETRIN A. - LEVINSOHN J., *Measuring Aggregate Productivity Growth Using Plant-level Data*, Mimeo, 2006.

SMARZYNSKA JAVORCIK B., «Does Foreign Direct Investment Increase the Productivity of Domestic Firms? In Search of Spillovers Through Backward Linkages», *American Economic Review*, vol. 94, 2004, pages 605-627.

187

Vertical Specialisation in Europe: Evidence from the Import Content of Exports

Emanuele Breda - Rita Cappariello - Roberta Zizza*

Banca d'Italia, Rome

We use input-output tables to estimate the import content (IC) of exports for several European countries, interpreting it as a measure of internationalisation. Between 1995 and 2000 the IC grew everywhere but in France; the transport equipment sector emerges as the most internationalised one. Italy and Germany show very different patterns, although both started from a very low level of IC. Italy experienced the weakest growth whereas Germany the most sizeable rise. We argue that Italian firms might have felt a lower pressure to transform their organisation due to the delayed effects of the 1992 and 1995 Lira crises. [JEL Classification: F14, C67]

1. - Introduction

One of the consequences of global market integration is the international fragmentation of production, *i.e.* the localisation

* <*emanuele.breda@bancaditalia.it*>; <*rita.cappariello@bancaditalia.it*>; Economic and Financial Statistics Department; <*roberta.zizza@bancaditalia.it*>; Department for Structural Economic Analysis. The Authors wish to thank, for their useful comments and suggestions, Alessandra De Michele, Stefano Federico, Marco Magnani, Paola Monti, Luigi Federico Signorini, Roberto Tedeschi, Francesco Zollino and seminar participants at the 47th Meeting of the *Società italiana degli economisti* (October 2006, Verona), the 16th International Input-Output Conference (July 2007, Istanbul) and the 9th European Trade Study Group Conference (September 2007, Athens). The views expressed in this paper are those of the authors and do not necessarily reflect those of the Banca d'Italia.

abroad of phases of production which previously took place in the home country.[1] This process reflects the firms' organisational choices aimed at reducing costs and increasing productivity on international markets (Antràs and Helpman, 2003; Helpman, 2006).

Vertical fragmentation of production takes place mainly in two ways, outsourcing and off-shoring. Outsourcing refers to firms giving up stages of their intermediate production chains and, consequently, buying parts from foreign suppliers; off-shoring refers to the establishment or acquisition of plants abroad to produce intermediate goods and services. An important role in this process has been played by the progress in the field of information and communication technologies, which makes it possible to reduce the coordination costs emerging when production is divided into separate stages (Jones and Kierzkowski, 2001).

Over the last decades world trade has grown faster than world GDP and manufacturing value added; intra-industry trade in final and intermediate goods accounts for a large part of trade growth, signalling the rising importance of the international fragmentation of production. Many empirical works — although non-homogeneous in terms of definitions, measures adopted and kind of data utilized — find evidence of the growing importance of vertical integration in the main industrialised countries. Feenstra and Hanson (1996), by using input-output tables, estimate that in the United States the share of imported inputs on the total purchase of intermediate products grew from 5.5 per cent in 1972 to 11.6 in 1990. Hummels et al. (1998, 2001) find evidence of an increasing share of imported goods and services content in exports for some OECD countries during the final part of the last century. The European Central Bank (2005a) estimates an increase of the

---

[1] Many different terms have been used in the literature for this phenomenon: outsourcing (FEENSTRA R.C. - HANSON G.H., 1996), international fragmentation of production (JONES R.W. - KIERZKOWSKI H., 2001), vertical specialisation (HUMMELS D. et AL., 2001; GOH A.T. - OLIVIER J., 2004), delocalisation (LEAMER E., 1998), vertical production networks (HANSON G.H. et AL., 2005), production sharing (FEENSTRA R.C., 1998). We will use them interchangeably.

import content of exports from 1995 to 2000 for a subset of euro area countries. For Italy, Breda *et* al. (2006) find an increase of the import content of exports between 1995 and 2000, while the import content declined between 1990 and 2000 according to ISAE (2005). Other empirical works focus instead on the effects of internationalisation of production on labour market developments (Feenstra and Hanson, 1996 and 1999; Amiti and Wei, 2004; Hijzen *et* al., 2004) or on output and value added volatility (Bergin *et* al., 2006).

This paper aims at comparing the value of imported goods and services embodied in exports by industry for a set of European countries. The measures we use were originally proposed by Hummels, Ishii and Yi (2001) (HIY, henceforth) to capture the concept of "vertical specialisation", *i.e.* when a good is produced in multiple stages across at least two countries, with each country participating in a separate stage of the good's production sequence and then exporting the good-in-process to the next country. These synthetic indicators of the degree of internationalisation of production include imports of intermediate inputs from both foreign affiliates and foreign suppliers (*i.e., direct* import content), as well as imports that are already incorporated in the capital and intermediate inputs acquired from domestic suppliers (*i.e., indirect* import content). The import content of exports is estimated from the information on production processes provided by the intersectoral tables (input-output tables) at current prices published, for Italy, by the Italian National Institute of Statistics (Istat) for years 1995 and 2000 (see Istat, 2006) and collected and published, for the other EU countries, by Eurostat.

The paper is organised as follows. In Section 2 the measure of the import content of exports is defined and the methodology for its estimate is introduced. Results for some European countries are presented and compared in Section 3, with a focus on Germany and Italy. An analysis by sector is presented in Section 4. Finally, Section 5 resumes the main results.

2. - The Import Content of Export: Concepts and Measures

There are two main ways in which firms internationalise their production process: foreign direct investments and outsourcing, *i.e.*, the purchase of intermediate inputs from foreign firms.[2] As in HIY, the measure of *vertical specialisation* we adopt is based on the idea that countries link sequentially to produce goods. We therefore focus on imported intermediate goods and services used by a country to make goods or services which are later exported to another country, irrespective of the relationship the domestic firm has established with the foreign supplier.

As an indicator of vertical specialisation we choose the import content (*IC*) of exports, calculated on the basis of the input-output tables.[3] Using these tables helps avoiding an arbitrary classification between intermediate inputs and other categories of goods: they allow us to disentangle the output of each sector into two parts, the first representing inputs to the other sectors, the second representing goods which satisfy the final demand. Obviously, they do not account for the international outsourcing to foreign subsidiaries of the whole production and distribution process (*export platform*), as this case neither implies flows of goods and services across home country borders, nor a change in the import content of exports.

Following HIY, in order to calculate the value of imports directly contained in the exports we resort to the following formula, here reported using matrix notation:

$$(1) \qquad direct\ IC\ of\ exports = IC\_dir = u_M A \cdot EXP$$

where u is a unit vector of dimension n, $_M A$ is an n-dimensional square matrix containing the production coefficients for imported

---

[2] PISCITELLO L. - TAJOLI L. (2005) show that for Italy there exists a positive relationship between different kinds of internationalisation in a given sector on a given market; they do not substitute one another and they tend to strengthen mutually.

[3] For each product in the economy, the tables indicate the intermediate inputs involved in the production (classified according to their origin, either foreign or domestic), the imports of the product itself as well as the uses of the product to satisfy the different components of the final demand (private and public consumption, investment, exports).

inputs, *EXP* is the *n*-vector of exports, with *n* being the number of sectors. Each element $a_{i,j}^M$ of the matrix $_M A$ measures the value of imported intermediate goods and services classified in the branch *i* and used to produce one unit of output in sector *j* (see Guarini and Tassinari, 1993).

Using the input-output tables allows us to calculate also the value of inputs which are *indirectly* employed in the production of an exported good. An imported input can indeed be used in a sector whose output is in turn employed in another sector, then possibly in a third sector and so on, to be eventually included in a good sold abroad. In this case the measure of the import content of exports includes both directly and indirectly imported inputs, the latter being defined as those contained in domestic inputs. The measure for the whole import content is the following:

$$(2) \qquad IC \; of \; exports = IC = u \, _M A (I - \, _D A)^{-1} EXP$$

where $_D A$ is the matrix of the input coefficients for domestic intermediate goods and $(I - _D A)^{-1}$ is the term capturing imported inputs embodied in the domestic output in the first, second, third, etc. stages of production before being used to produce the good that will eventually be exported.

3. - Vertical Specialisation in Europe. A Whole-Economy, Cross-Country Comparison

3.1 *Data Sources*

The analysis on vertical specialisation is based on symmetrical input-output tables, which are compiled approximately every five years by the EU national statistical agencies and collected by Eurostat. For Italy, the tables used are those recently released by Istat and compiled according to a new methodology which guarantees more consistency between intersectoral transactions and national accounts statistics, making it possible to quantify domestic and international outsourcing using *direct* data on imported and domestically produced goods and services (see Bracci, 2006).

The symmetrical tables distinguish between intermediate purchases from domestic suppliers (the so-called "domestic matrix") and imported intermediate purchases ("import matrix"). The latest available tables for a representative set of countries are at current prices and refer to years 1995 and 2000. Tables at current prices do not allow telling apart the effects due to a variation in technical coefficients for domestic and imported inputs from the effects due to a change in relative prices. We chose, however, not to deflate the aggregates derived from the tables since detailed and reliable data on export and import prices are not currently available for all countries.

We provide a measure of the import content of exports for seven European countries: six Monetary Union members (Belgium, France, Germany, Italy, the Netherlands and Spain) and the United Kingdom. This panel of countries currently accounts for about 82 per cent of the EU-25 GDP and 76 per cent of trade in goods and services (86 and 82 per cent, respectively, of the EU-15 GDP and trade). The input-output tables provide a sectoral breakdown into fifty-nine sectors (according to the CPA classification), twenty-two of which are manufacturing sectors.[4] The development of the phenomenon of vertical specialisation in the course of the second half of the 1990s will also be measured for an aggregate of EMU members only, due to the unavailability of input-output tables for the United Kingdom in 2000.

3.2 *Differences and Similarities in the Extent of Internationalisation*

Table 1 shows three different indicators of the import content

---

[4] The international comparison is obviously more reliable if input-output tables with the same sectoral disaggregation are available. However, since for France no homogeneous tables are published for the two considered years, we use input-output tables from different sources. The 1995 table provides data which are broken down into 40 industries from the ISIC Rev 3 classification, whereas the 2000 table is broken down into 59 products from the CPA classification. Although the mismatch between the two classifications does not allow sectoral comparisons between the two periods, we still consider meaningful to compare the aggregate results for France in the two years.

Table 1

IMPORT CONTENT OF EXPORTS BY SECTOR OF THE MAIN
EU COUNTRIES
(percentage values)

Countries	Year	Whole economy	Manufacturing	Whole economy, including transit trade
Italy	1995	24.4	27.5	24.7
	2000	27.2	30.6	27.8
Germany	1995	21.5	23.9	29.4
	2000	27.9	31.0	37.9
Netherlands	1995	33.8	42.6	50.0
	2000	37.3	48.1	56.6
Belgium	1995	41.5	49.9	55.2
	2000	46.6	54.3	60.4
France	1995[1]	20.5	23.7	26.8
	2000	20.5	24.5	41.3
United Kingdom	1995	23.0	28.4	26.1
	2000	-	-	–
Spain	1995	27.5	33.5	27.5
	2000	34.9	42.9	34.9

Source: Authors' calculations on Eurostat and, for Italy, Istat data.
[1] The 1995 results for France are based on OECD input-output tables with a different sectoral classification. See also footnote 4 in the text.

of exports. The first one measures the overall (direct and indirect) import content of goods and services produced in the country and then exported; the second one regards manufactured goods only. The third one is a broader measure of internationalisation, which includes 'transit trade', *i.e.* goods imported in the declaring country and thereafter directly re-exported without any transformation.

The overall IC of exports emerges as being quite heterogeneous across countries. In 1995 it ranged between 22 and 42 per cent, with lower-end values characterising larger countries

(France, Germany) and upper-end values characterising smaller countries (the Netherlands and Belgium). Five years later the ranking remains broadly the same, although no observation can be made for the UK. The IC grew between 1995 and 2000 in all countries considered but France; Spain and Germany experienced the strongest growth of import content in relative terms, with the latter country starting from a very low level in 1995. In 2000 the IC of exports was equal to about 27-28 per cent in Italy and Germany; it was 35 per cent in Spain, while in Belgium and the Netherlands the phenomenon was much more pronounced (47 and 37 per cent, respectively). When aggregating across the six members of the Monetary Union by using the export-weighted average of each country's indicator, we observe an increase in the average import content of domestically produced exports from 25.5 to 30.0 per cent (29.5 per cent by keeping country export weights constant at 1995 level), largely reflecting the upward trend in vertical specialisation recorded in Germany.[5]

We claim this change is quite dramatic as the growth of the IC of exports we detect in a 5-year period (4.5 percentage points) overcomes that estimated by HIY over a 20-year period, from 1970 to 1990 (3.6 percentage points), for a partially overlapping set of OECD countries.

The growing intensity of vertical specialisation in Germany is confirmed by other indicators as well. For instance, the share of "own" (*i.e.*, domestically produced) value added in the German manufacturing sector declined sharply in the second half of the 1990s, at a higher rate than in the other EU countries[6]. Sinn (2004, 2006) argues that Germany's high wages and rigid labour·market stimulated a wave of international relocation of production (especially in the automotive sector and towards the neighbouring Eastern European countries that would have later joined the EU),[7] leaving in Germany almost only the final stages of production,

---

[5] Countries are aggregated without netting the intra-trade.
[6] See SINN H.-W. (2006, figure 3).
[7] See "The impact of FDI in import structure" in BUNDESBANK (2006, pages 54-55).

which are usually more capital and skill intensive. This is the so-called "bazaar effect": to simplify, German firms export basic components and raw materials to their foreign affiliates located in lower-wage countries, assemble (almost) entirely their products abroad and re-import them to implement the final stages of production, "put the brand" and sell the final goods in domestic and foreign markets. This phenomenon generates a surge in international trade flows and, thanks to cost competitiveness gains, is likely to trigger a positive performance of exports market shares and current account balance; however, because of the lower domestically generated value added, this does not necessarily stimulate GDP growth.[8]

In the same period (1995-2000), on the contrary, the internationalisation of Italian production was just at its beginning: the Lira devaluation in 1992 and its depreciation in 1995 had temporarily boosted the price competitiveness of Italian goods, making the re-organisation of production processes plausibly less urgent. Between the end of the last decade and the beginning of the current one, many factors made the re-organisation of production much more compelling for Italian manufacturing firms.[9] Among these factors were the waning effects of the Lira crises on price competitiveness and the adoption of the Euro that, once and for all, eliminated exchange rate fluctuations for almost half of the Italian external trade, as well as the aggressive entry into world markets of low labour cost emerging countries, such as China and India. All these elements increased, above all, the competitive pressure on Italian "traditional" products (textiles and clothing, leather and footwear, furniture etc.). Further competitiveness losses were caused by the appreciation of the Euro during 2001-04 and by decreasing labour productivity. It later became clear that the model of the industrial districts, successfully implemented especially during the 1990s and quite widespread in

---

[8] See also DANNINGER F. - JOUTZ S. (2007). For critical or different views about the "bazaar economy" argument, see BECHERT S. - CELLARIUS G. (2004) and BELKE A. *et* AL. (2007).

[9] PISCITELLO L. - TAJOLI L. (2005) find some evidence of a process of internationalisation of production for Italian firms in more recent years.

that kind of productions, had to be rethought in face of the increasing globalisation.[10] The lag Italy showed in the internationalisation process could be arguably put in connection also with structural factors, such as the predominance of small and medium enterprises and the lower diffusion of information and communication technologies with respect to the main European countries (OECD, 2004).

This stylised picture for the period 1995-2000 - Italy started from a relatively low level of internationalisation of production and the phenomenon grew less than in the other EU countries, while Germany started from a relatively low level too, but experienced a growth rate above the average - is confirmed, at least for the share of international outsourcing implemented via direct investment activity, by the *ratio* between outward FDI stock and GDP. In Italy this indicator rose only from 9.0 per cent in 1995 to 16.4 per cent in 2000, widening the negative gap with respect to all the other countries analysed, while in Germany it started from the third lowest level (10.8 per cent) and almost tripled (up to 29.0 per cent). Spain's FDI stock to GDP *ratio*, probably due also to catching-up effects, experienced the most exceptional growth (from 5.9 to 29.6 per cent). In the other EU countries analysed the same indicator started from higher levels and more than doubled: in France it grew from 13.5 to 34.0 per cent, in the United Kingdom from 26.5 to 62.4 per cent, in Belgium (plus Luxembourg) from 27.8 to 72.5 per cent and in the Netherlands from 41.1 to 82.4 per cent.[11]

According to the broader measure of internationalisation, which includes 'transit trade', the IC of exports for the six EMU countries reached 41.7 per cent in 2000, from 33.5 in 1995. The figure for year 2000 compares with that estimated by the

---

[10] Some districts, e.g. North-East textile and shoe manufacturers, switched from a "traditional district model" (headquarters and manufacturing facilities in the same geographic area) to a "new value chain model" (headquarters in Italy, manufacturing facilities in countries with lower labour costs; see OECD, 2004). For some case studies, see AMIGHINI A. - RABELOTTI R. (2003); BENTIVOGLI C. - SCINTILLANI L. (2004).

[11] See UNCTAD (2005); for Italy, own calculations on Banca d'Italia - UIC and Istat data.

European Central Bank (2005*a*) for a slightly different subset of countries (44.2 per cent).[12]

The measure including transit trade shows an even higher variability across countries than the one excluding it. Transit trade is negligible for Italy and Spain, while it is extremely sizeable for the Netherlands and Belgium, due also to their size and geographical position. The developments for the manufacturing sector alone are quite similar to those referring to the whole economy.

3.3 *The Rise in Oil Price: Is it the Whole Story?*

In the period 1995-2000 the oil price, expressed in US dollars, rose by more than 64 per cent. Since we use input-output tables at current prices, our results are likely to be affected, at least partly, by the nominal growth of energy imports that "mechanically" inflated the IC. According to Eurostat trade statistics, between 1995 and 2000 the share of energy products on total imports grew by more than two percentage points in all the EMU countries considered: from 7.3 to 9.7 per cent in Italy, from 6.2 to 8.8 per cent in Germany, from 5.9 to 8.9 per cent in Belgium, from 8.3 to 10.6 per cent in the Netherlands, from 6.3 to 8.9 per cent in France and from 8.0 to 12.1 per cent in Spain. So, in order to eliminate the oil price effect, we calculate the IC of exports excluding energy minerals from imports and also excluding completely the energy input both in its domestic and imported components.

If we exclude energy products or sectors (Table 2), IC growth is still confirmed but, to a varying extent, less pronounced in all EMU countries but France where, as stated above, data at sectoral level are not fully comparable between 1995 and 2000. For Belgium and, in particular, for Germany both level and variation of IC are only slightly reduced by the exclusion of energy. For

---

[12] The countries considered are Austria, Finland, Germany, Italy and the Netherlands. Also in the ECB's exercise the countries are aggregated without netting the intra-trade.

TABLE 2

IMPORT CONTENT OF EXPORTS OF THE MAIN EU COUNTRIES
EXCLUDING ENERGY
(percentage values)

Countries	Year	Net of imported energy minerals	Net of energy sector
Italy	1995	23.6	22.4
	2000	25.4	24.2
Germany	1995	20.3	19.5
	2000	26.2	24.9
Netherlands	1995	30.4	30.1
	2000	31.2	31.1
Belgium	1995	39.8	37.2
	2000	44.1	40.7
France	1995 [1]	20.2	19.4
	2000	18.3	17.8
United Kingdom	1995	22.5	22.6
	2000	–	–
Spain	1995	25.9	24.7
	2000	31.8	29.9

Source: Authors' calculations on Eurostat and, for Italy, Istat data.
[1] The 1995 results for France are obtained by utilising the OECD input-output tables with a different sectorial classification. See also footnote 4 in the text.

Italy, and even more so for the Netherlands, both the absolute levels and the 1995-2000 growth are significantly lower. In Italy the IC of total exports net of imported energy inputs grew from 23.6 to 25.4 per cent (by 7.9 per cent; see Table 2, first column), in the Netherlands from 30.4 to 31.2 (by 2.7 per cent). When including energy minerals, the two countries' IC of total exports grew, respectively, by 11.6 and 10.5 per cent (see Table 1, second column).

4. - The Degree of Internationalisation by Industry

Averaging on the five available countries, between 1995 and 2000 all manufacturing branches experienced a growth in the IC of exports (Graph 1).

In 2000 the degree of internationalisation in the transport equipment sector was particularly high in all the countries, ranging between 29 and 66 per cent, well above the average for manufacturing (Table 3). Due to its highly standardised production process, this is a typical sector in which international vertical specialisation is widely adopted.

Also in the chemical sector the degree of international fragmentation of production seems particularly high in all

GRAPH 1

IMPORT CONTENT OF EXPORTS BY SECTOR IN A FIVE-COUNTRY AGGREGATE IN YEARS 1995 AND 2000 [1]
(percentage values)

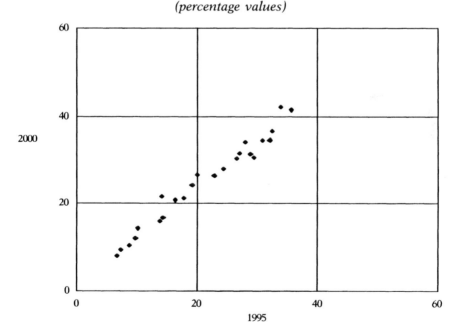

Source: Authors' calculations on Eurostat and, for Italy, Istat data.
[1] Belgium, Germany, Italy, the Netherlands, Spain.

201

TABLE 3

IMPORT CONTENT OF EXPORTS BY SECTOR IN SOME EMU COUNTRIES
(percentage values)

Sectors	Italy		Germany		Netherlands		Belgium		France		Spain	
	1995	2000	1995	2000	1995	2000	1995	2000	1995	2000	1995	2000
Products of agriculture, forestry and fishing	7.4	8.3	11.8	15.1	17.7	19.8	25.7	27.2	-	13.2	11.1	13.8
Energy minerals	10.7	23.2	10.6	16.6	8.4	9.8	-	24.2	-	14.5	7.1	21.8
Non-energy minerals	13.9	16.4	11.4	16.6	19.5	22.2	25.2	28.8	-	18.1	11.2	20.8
Manufactures	27.5	30.6	23.9	31.0	42.6	48.1	49.9	54.3	23.7	24.5	33.5	42.9
Food products, beverages and tobacco	19.1	19.8	19.2	21.0	38.0	38.9	41.7	43.5	-	15.6	19.7	26.4
Textile products and clothing	24.5	28.0	30.6	36.2	50.6	48.7	47.8	51.1	-	24.6	30.9	36.0
Leather and leather products	25.7	30.2	32.4	38.3	36.7	39.0	47.0	53.3	-	21.7	26.4	32.3
Wood and wood products	22.5	24.9	14.9	19.5	39.3	39.7	39.7	46.5	-	15.6	22.7	33.8
Paper and paper products, printing and publishing	26.7	27.9	23.8	27.0	39.5	40.1	42.4	45.7	-	21.6	29.3	34.8
Refined petroleum products	49.7	69.7	72.6	81.2	74.5	80.8	63.5	83.4	-	51.3	59.7	73.6
Chemical products and man-made fibres	38.9	42.0	23.4	34.7	42.3	51.0	49.7	52.6	-	21.7	31.4	47.0
Rubber and plastic products	32.6	34.4	24.2	29.5	45.4	44.6	45.1	47.6	-	22.7	36.2	36.4
Non-metallic mineral products	18.0	20.1	12.0	16.6	27.2	28.4	30.4	36.5	-	13.9	12.1	18.5
Basic metals and metal products	28.5	29.9	28.0	34.1	37.6	40.1	51.4	56.1	-	29.1	25.7	31.6
Mechanical machinery and equipment	23.6	25.0	19.0	24.1	37.9	39.9	45.1	43.0	-	18.7	24.3	30.0
Electrical equipment and precision instruments	31.7	34.3	20.9	28.1	42.2	47.9	44.5	50.9	-	24.6	32.8	41.9

(continued on next page)

(*continued*) Table 3

IMPORT CONTENT OF EXPORTS BY SECTOR IN SOME EMU COUNTRIES
(*percentage values*)

Sectors	Italy		Germany		Netherlands		Belgium		France		Spain	
	1995	2000	1995	2000	1995	2000	1995	2000	1995	2000	1995	2000
Transport equipment	31.2	34.4	27.6	35.0	50.0	52.3	62.1	66.2	-	29.2	45.5	55.7
Other manufactures	27.4	28.7	20.9	26.3	24.2	26.9	43.3	56.2	-	17.0	22.4	29.4
Electricity, gas and water	24.4	32.5	8.3	13.5	13.6	20.1	20.5	25.2	-	21.0	14.5	32.0
Construction	12.2	13.1	10.8	14.6	25.6	25.6	21.6	28.2	-		13.1	18.1
Wholesale and retail trade	10.3	12.0	5.7	9.3	16.6	17.4	13.6	28.5	-	5.3	5.9	9.8
Hotels and restaurant	11.8	11.2	12.0	14.3	18.2	19.1	20.5	24.0	-		-	-
Transport and communication	13.4	15.8	18.7	24.5	25.8	29.8	26.4	39.4	-	10.5	15.6	25.3
Financial intermediation	5.1	5.6	7.9	10.3	6.3	7.4	10.5	15.9	-	5.6	4.6	8.1
Real estate, renting and business activities, consulting	8.7	9.1	4.7	6.7	14.2	14.2	17.0	21.6	-	6.3	7.7	12.3
Public administration and services to households	4.7	5.4	4.7	6.5	9.0	9.7	5.4	10.2	-	5.5	6.1	8.2
Total	24.4	27.2	21.5	27.9	33.8	37.3	41.5	46.6	20.5	20.5	27.5	34.9
Total including transit trade	24.7	27.8	29.4	37.9	50.0	56.6	55.2	60.4	26.8	41.3	27.5	34.9

Source: Authors' calculations on Eurostat and, for Italy, Istat data. See footnote 4 in the text for French data.

countries with the exception of France. The IC of exports for low-tech sectors such as "textile products and clothing" and "leather and leather products" is in line with the average for manufacturing everywhere but in Germany; for Italy, which is strongly specialised in these sectors, this seems to corroborate the findings according to which producing abroad was not so pronounced, at least until 2000.

In the two main service sectors, *i.e.* "transport and communication" and "wholesale and retail trade", the IC turns out to be quite lower than in the manufacturing sector for all the countries.

The variation of import requirement between 1995 and 2000 was broken down into two parts according to the standard shift and share analysis. The first part accounts for the change in the intensity of IC within each sector; the second part for the change in the sectoral composition of exports (Table 4). The increase in the intensity of import content explains 95 per cent of the whole variation in the five-country aggregate; the branches providing the highest contributions to IC growth of exports are "chemical products and man-made fibres", "transport equipment" and "electrical equipment and precision instruments". The change in the sectoral composition is found to play a marginal role (Table 5).

5. - Conclusions

Following the methodology developed by HIY, this paper measures and compares the extent of vertical specialisation for a set of European countries, proxied by the import content of exports. This indicator is aimed at taking into account the linkages of production processes in a vertical trading chain across countries.

Our evidence supports a significant increase between 1995 and 2000 in the vertical specialisation of the countries considered, fairly comparable in terms of magnitude with that detected over a 20-year period by HIY. In the 5-year period the import content

TABLE 4

DECOMPOSITION BY SECTOR OF THE GROWTH OF THE IMPORT CONTENT OF EXPORTS IN FIVE EMU COUNTRIES

(percentage values)

Sectors	Italy			Germany			Netherlands		
	Contribution to the growth of IC of total exports	Change in the intensity of IC within each sector	Change in the sectoral composition of exports	Contribution to the growth of IC of total exports	Change in the intensity of IC within each sector	Change in the sectoral composition of exports	Contribution to the growth of IC of total exports	Change in the intensity of IC within each sector	Change in the sectoral composition of exports
Products of agriculture, forestry and fishing	-0.01	0.01	-0.02	0.00	0.03	-0.03	-0.12	0.12	-0.24
Energy minerals	0.00	0.00	0.00	0.00	0.01	-0.01	0.06	0.04	0.02
Non-energy minerals	0.00	0.00	0.00	0.00	0.01	-0.01	0.02	0.01	0.01
Manufactures	2.62	2.01	0.61	5.64	5.54	0.10	2.62	2.42	0.20
Food products, beverages and tobacco	-0.01	0.03	-0.04	-0.03	0.07	-0.09	-1.12	0.15	-1.27
Textile products and clothing	0.08	0.31	-0.24	-0.10	0.12	-0.21	-0.21	-0.03	-0.18
Leather and leather products	0.11	0.19	-0.08	0.00	0.02	-0.02	-0.01	0.00	-0.01
Wood and wood products	0.01	0.01	0.00	0.04	0.02	0.02	-0.03	0.00	-0.03
Paper and paper products, printing and publishing	-0.01	0.02	-0.03	0.09	0.11	-0.02	-0.23	0.02	-0.25
Refined petroleum products	0.68	0.18	0.50	0.28	0.06	0.22	2.09	0.30	1.79
Chemical products and man-made fibres	0.72	0.23	0.49	1.24	1.35	-0.11	0.81	1.26	-0.45
Rubber and plastic products	0.04	0.06	-0.02	0.17	0.16	0.00	-0.10	-0.02	-0.08
Non-metallic mineral products	0.01	0.07	-0.06	0.04	0.06	-0.02	-0.05	0.01	-0.06
Basic metals and metal products	-0.13	0.11	-0.23	0.26	0.52	-0.26	-0.12	0.13	-0.24

(continued on next page)

205

(continued) TABLE 4

DECOMPOSITION BY SECTOR OF THE GROWTH OF THE IMPORT CONTENT OF EXPORTS IN FIVE EMU COUNTRIES
(percentage values)

Sectors	Italy			Germany			Netherlands		
	Contribution to the growth of IC of total exports	Change in the intensity of IC within each sector	Change in the sectoral composition of exports	Contribution to the growth of IC of total exports	Change in the intensity of IC within each sector	Change in the sectoral composition of exports	Contribution to the growth of IC of total exports	Change in the intensity of IC within each sector	Change in the sectoral composition of exports
Mechanical machinery and equipment	0.19	0.23	-0.04	0.34	0.72	-0.38	0.42	0.08	0.34
Electrical equipment and precision instruments	0.35	0.22	0.14	1.14	0.82	0.32	0.80	0.39	0.41
Transport equipment	0.50	0.28	0.22	2.11	1.43	0.68	0.33	0.11	0.22
Other manufactures	0.07	0.07	0.00	0.05	0.08	-0.02	0.02	0.02	0.00
Electricity, gas and water	0.00	0.00	0.00	0.00	0.01	0.00	0.00	0.01	-0.01
Construction	-0.01	0.00	-0.02	0.00	0.00	0.00	0.02	0.00	0.02
Wholesale and retail trade	0.14	0.12	0.02	0.23	0.21	0.02	0.17	0.08	0.09
Hotels and restaurant	0.00	0.00	0.00	0.02	0.01	0.01	0.00	0.00	0.00
Transport and communication	0.00	0.13	-0.13	0.36	0.34	0.01	0.47	0.45	0.02
Financial intermediation	0.00	0.00	0.00	0.01	0.01	0.00	0.04	0.01	0.03
Real estate, renting, business activities	0.07	0.01	0.06	0.10	0.07	0.03	0.26	0.00	0.26
Public administration, services to households	0.00	0.00	0.00	0.01	0.01	0.00	0.00	0.01	-0.01
Total	2.83	2.30	0.53	6.37	6.25	0.12	3.54	3.14	0.40

(continued on next page)

206

(continued) Table 4

DECOMPOSITION BY SECTOR OF THE GROWTH OF THE IMPORT CONTENT OF EXPORTS IN FIVE EMU COUNTRIES
(percentage values)

Sectors	Belgium			Spain		
	Contribution to the growth of IC of total exports	Change in the intensity of IC within each sector	Change in the sectoral composition of exports	Contribution to the growth of IC of total exports	Change in the intensity of IC within each sector	Change in the sectoral composition of exports
Products of agriculture, forestry and fishing	-0.03	0.01	-0.04	-0.02	0.15	-0.18
Energy minerals	0.00	0.00	0.00	0.00	0.00	0.00
Non-energy minerals	-0.03	0.02	-0.04	0.03	0.04	-0.01
Manufactures	1.34	3.09	-1.75	5.60	6.32	-0.71
Food products, beverages and tobacco	-0.27	0.15	-0.42	0.30	0.41	-0.11
Textile products and clothing	-0.26	0.14	-0.40	0.05	0.15	-0.10
Leather and leather products	-0.03	0.01	-0.05	0.02	0.10	-0.09
Wood and wood products	0.06	0.05	0.01	0.07	0.07	0.01
Paper and paper products, printing and publishing	0.24	0.07	0.17	0.08	0.13	-0.05
Refined petroleum products	1.63	0.66	0.97	1.27	0.38	0.89
Chemical products and man-made fibres	0.48	0.42	0.05	0.82	1.16	-0.33
Rubber and plastic products	-0.07	0.07	-0.14	-0.09	0.01	-0.09
Non-metallic mineral products	0.03	0.12	-0.09	0.10	0.17	-0.07
Basic metals and metal products	-0.41	0.48	-0.89	0.12	0.40	-0.28
Mechanical machinery and equipment	-0.19	-0.09	-0.10	0.37	0.32	0.05
Electrical equipment and precision instruments	0.96	0.32	0.64	0.74	0.65	0.09
Transport equipment	-1.06	0.48	-1.54	1.60	2.24	-0.65
Other manufactures	0.25	0.21	0.04	0.15	0.12	0.03
Electricity, gas and water	0.06	0.01	0.05	0.02	0.01	0.01
Construction	0.03	0.03	0.01	0.00	0.00	0.00

(continued on next page)

(*continued*) TABLE 4

DECOMPOSITION BY SECTOR OF THE GROWTH OF THE IMPORT CONTENT OF EXPORTS
IN FIVE EMU COUNTRIES
(*percentage values*)

Sectors	Belgium			Spain		
	Contribution to the growth of IC of total exports	Change in the intensity of IC within each sector	Change in the sectoral composition of exports	Contribution to the growth of IC of total exports	Change in the intensity of IC within each sector	Change in the sectoral composition of exports
Wholesale and retail trade	1.45	1.31	0.15	0.28	0.24	0.04
Hotels and restaurant	0.02	0.03	-0.01	-	-	-
Transport and communication	1.50	1.08	0.42	0.89	0.74	0.16
Financial intermediation	0.08	0.08	0.00	0.11	0.05	0.07
Real estate, renting, business activities	0.64	0.32	0.32	0.46	0.26	0.20
Public administration, services to households	0.01	0.02	-0.01	0.02	0.01	0.02
Total	5.09	5.99	-0.90	7.40	7.81	-0.40

Source: Authors' calculations on Eurostat and, for Italy, Istat data.

Table 5

DECOMPOSITION BY SECTOR OF THE GROWTH OF THE IMPORT
CONTENT OF EXPORTS BETWEEN 1995 AND 2000
IN A FIVE-COUNTRY AGGREGATE [1]
(percentage values)

Sectors	Contribution to the growth of IC of total exports	Change in the intensity of IC within each sector	Change in the sectoral composition of exports
Products of agriculture, forestry and fishing	-0.02	0.04	-0.06
Energy minerals	0.01	0.01	0.00
Non-energy minerals	0.00	0.01	-0.01
Manufactures	4.06	3.90	0.16
Food products, beverages and tobacco	-0.21	0.07	-0.28
Textile products and clothing	-0.11	0.14	-0.25
Leather and leather products	0.01	0.06	-0.05
Wood and wood products	0.03	0.02	0.01
Paper and paper products, printing and publishing	0.04	0.07	-0.03
Refined petroleum products	0.88	0.20	0.67
Chemical products and man-made fibres	0.89	0.94	-0.05
Rubber and plastic products	0.04	0.08	-0.03
Non-metallic mineral products	0.02	0.07	-0.05
Basic metals and metal products	0.03	0.33	-0.31
Mechanical machinery and equipment	0.21	0.42	-0.20
Electrical equipment and precision instruments	0.85	0.55	0.30
Transport equipment	1.32	0.86	0.46
Other manufactures	0.06	0.09	-0.03
Electricity, gas and water	0.01	0.01	0.00
Construction	0.00	0.01	-0.01
Wholesale and retail trade	0.33	0.29	0.04
Hotels and restaurant	0.01	0.01	0.00
Transport and communication	0.47	0.46	0.01
Financial intermediation	0.03	0.02	0.01
Real estate, renting and business activities, consulting	0.22	0.10	0.12
Public administration and services to households	0.01	0.01	0.00
Total	5.13	4.85	0.27

Source: Authors' calculations on Eurostat and, for Italy, Istat data.
[1] Belgium, Germany, Italy, the Netherlands, Spain.

209

of exports grew in Belgium, Germany, Italy, the Netherlands and Spain; results for France are less clear-cut due to underlying data which are non-fully comparable across time. The production of transport equipment emerges as the most internationalised sector. However, two of the biggest countries in this group show very different patterns: Italy started in 1995 from the second lowest level of IC and experienced the weakest growth (11.6 per cent, considering total exports); Germany started from the lowest level of IC but experienced by far the most sizeable rise (29.6 per cent).

Plausibly, at the beginning of the period, Italian firms felt a lower pressure to transform their organisation by locating segments of their production process abroad, due to the delayed effects on price competitiveness of the 1992 and 1995 Lira crises; only later Italian products, especially the "traditional" ones, started suffering from rising competition from developing countries and weak growth of world demand. Then it became clear that the model of industrial districts, particularly common in that kind of productions, had to be rethought in the light of the globalisation process. Also other structural issues, such as the small size of firms and low diffusion of information and communication technology, possibly contributed to explain why Italy was lagging behind in the process of internationalisation.

In the second half of the 1990s, on the contrary, German firms were already experiencing an increasing competition on both domestic and foreign markets (also from Italian products), so they started a rapid process of international outsourcing of manufacturing activities, leaving in their home country basically only the final (and most capital and skill-intensive) stages of production as well as R&D and marketing activities. Drawing from this evidence, some economists and observers started to define Germany as a "bazaar economy".

BIBLIOGRAPHY

Amighini A. - Rabelotti R., «The Effects of Globalisation on Industrial Districts in Italy: Evidence from the Footwear Sector», *ERSA, Conference Papers*, no. 500, 2003.

Amiti M. - Wei S., «Fear of Service Outsourcing: Is it Justified?», Cambridge (MA), *NBER, Working Paper*, no. 10808, 2004.

Antràs P. - Helpman E., «Global Sourcing», Cambridge (MA), *NBER, Working Paper*, no. 10082, 2003.

Bechert S. - Cellarius G., «Outsourcing Offers a Chance for the Development of Strongly Competitive European Enterprises», *IFO, Schnelldienst*, no. 7/2004, 2004.

Belke A. - Mattes A. - Wang L., «The Bazaar Economy Hypothesis Revisited. A new Measure for Germany's International Openness», *Hohenheimer Diskussionbeiträge*, no. 285, 2007.

Bentivogli C. - Scintillani L., «Internazionalizzazione dei mercati, new economy e sviluppo locale: il distretto di Sassuolo negli anni '90», in Conigliani C. (eds.), *Tra sviluppo e stagnazione: l'economia dell'Emilia-Romagna*, Bologna, Il Mulino, 2004, pages 151-194.

Bergin P. - Feenstra R.C. - Hanson G.H., «Outsourcing and Volatility», paper presented at *NBER, Summer Institute on International trade and investment* (ITI), Cambridge (MA) 31/7-3/8/2006, 2006.

Bracci L., «Una misura della delocalizzazione internazionale», in Ice (eds.), *Rapporto sul commercio estero*, Rome, 2006.

Breda E. - Cappariello R. - Zizza R., *The Measures of the External Trade Impulse to Economic Growth: How Relevant is the Internationalization of Production?*, paper presented at the XLVII Meeting of the Società italiana degli economisti (SIE), Verona 27-28/10/2006, 2006.

Bundesbank, *Monthly Report*, Frankfurt am Main, September, 2006.

Danninger F. - Joutz S., «What Explains Germany's Rebounding Export Market Share?», Washington (DC), *IMF, Working paper*, no. 24, 2007.

Ecb, *Import Content of Euro Area Exports*, Frankfurt am Main, Mimeo, 2005a.

— —, «*Measure of the Export Impulse to Euro Area Growth: Should we Look at Net Trade or Exports?*», Frankfurt am Main, Mimeo, 2005b.

Feenstra R.C., «Integration of Trade and Disintegration of Production in the Global Economy», *Journal of Economic Perspectives*, vol. 12, 1998, pages 31-50.

Feenstra R.C. - Hanson G.H., «Globalization, Outsourcing, and Wage Inequality», *AEA, Papers and Proceedings*, vol. 86, 1996, pages 240-245.

— — - — —, «The Impact of Outsourcing and High-Technology Capital on Wages: Estimates for the United States, 1979-1990», *Quarterly Journal of Economics*, vol. 114, 1999, pages 907-940.

Goh A.T. - Olivier J., «International Vertical Specialization, Imperfect Competition and Welfare», *CEPR, Discussion Paper*, no. 4311, 2004.

Guarini R. - Tassinari F., *Statistica economica*, Bologna, Il Mulino, 1993.

Hanson G.H. - Mataloni Jr. R.J. - Slaughter M.J., «Vertical Production Networks in Multinational Firms», *Review of Economics and Statistics*, vol. 87, no. 4, 2005, pages 664-678.

Helpman E., «Trade, FDI, and the Organization of Firms», Cambridge (MA), *NBER, Working Paper*, no. 12091, 2006.

HIJZEN A. - GÖRG H. - HINE R.C., «International Outsourcing and the Skill Structure of Labour Demand in the United Kingdom», *IZA, Discussion Paper*, no. 1249, 2004.

HUMMELS D. - ISHII J. - YI K., «The Nature and Growth of Vertical Specialization in World Trade», *Journal of International Economics*, vol. 54, 2001, pages 75-96.

HUMMELS D. - RAPOPORT D. - YI K., «Vertical Specialization and the Changing Nature of World Trade», New York, *FRBNY, Economic Policy Review*, June, 1998, pages 79-98.

ISAE, *Il fabbisogno di importazioni delle componenti finali della domanda*, Rome, 2005.

ISTAT, *Il nuovo sistema input-output*, Rome, Mimeo, 2006.

JONES R.W. - KIERZKOWSKI H., «A Framework for Fragmentation», in ARNDT S.W. - KIERZKOWSKI H. (eds.), *Fragmentation. New Production Patterns in the World Economy*, Oxford, Oxford University Press, 2001.

LEAMER E., «In Search of Stolper-Samuelson Linkages Between International Trade and Lower Wages», in COLLINS M. (ed.), *Imports, Exports, and the American Worker*, Washington (DC), Brooking Institution, 1998.

OECD, «ICT Diffusion to Business. Peer Review. Country Report: Italy», Directorate for Science, Technology and Industry, *Working Party on the Information Economy*, Paris, 2004.

PISCITELLO L. - TAJOLI L., «Il modello di specializzazione italiano: un'analisi estesa a più forme di internazionalizzazione», *Economia e Politica Industriale*, no. 3, 2005.

SINN H.-W., «Bazaar Economy», *IFO - Viewpoint*, no. 50, 2004.

— —, «The Pathological Export Boom and the Bazaar Effect. How to Solve the German Puzzle», *Cesifo, Working Paper*, no. 1708, 2006.

UNCTAD, *World Investment Report: Transnational Corporations and the Internationalization of R&D*, New York, United Nations, 2005.

212